EASY TO MAKE
PAPIER MACHE

EASY TO MAKE

PAPIER MACHE

Lindy Tristram

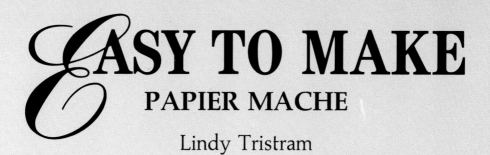

ANAYA PUBLISHERS LTD LONDON

For my Father

First published in Great Britain in 1993
by Anaya Publishers Ltd, Strode House,
44–50 Osnaburgh Street, London NW1 3ND

Editor Eve Harlow
Design by Design 23
Photography Steve Tanner
Illustrator Kate Simunek
Artwork Design 23

British Library Cataloguing in Publication Data

Tristram, Lindy
Easy to make papier mâché. – (Easy to make)
1. Papier mâché. 2. Crafts
1. Title 11. Series
745.54
ISBN 1 85470 120 7

Typeset by Servis Filmsetting Ltd, Manchester, UK
Colour Reproduction by Columbia Offset, Singapore
Printed and bound in Hong Kong

CONTENTS

Introduction

Papier mâché was developed nearly 300 years ago. Modern pastes and paints make it a simple craft that all the family can enjoy.

Paper, as we know it, was invented in China around AD 105, using the inner bark of the mulberry tree. Later, the Chinese had evolved ways of pounding other fibres to a pulp for paper – rags, hemp rope, discarded fishing nets, etc. Eventually, the art of paper making spread westwards to the Middle East, then to Europe.

The French were the first Europeans to develop papier mâché. In the early part of the 18th century vast quantities of waste paper accumulated in Paris as a result of the posters and notices that were put up and torn down almost nightly. Paper was expensive so a use had to be found for the waste. By mashing the paper in water, a pulp was produced and small articles such as snuff boxes and trinket boxes were moulded from the pulp. The British thought they could do better with the technique and a considerable papier mâché pulp industry, employing a great many people, built up in the north of England.

A new material

During the 18th century, beautiful lacquer work from the Far East was very popular and much sought after. British 'japanners' naturally wanted to take advantage of the demand but they were hampered by the materials available to them. The Chinese and Japanese craftsmen used a natural 'lacquer' which dried in the sun, so they could use wood as a body for their work. British lacquers and varnishes had to be 'stoved' or baked so wood was unsuitable as it warped or cracked under heat. A smooth-surfaced material was needed which could be decorated and lacquered in a similar style to that of the Chinese and Japanese but one that could also withstand 'stoving'.

In 1772, Henry Clay, a japanner from Birmingham in the north of England, invented a process that answered the problem – layered paper. Clay's process was simple – sheets of paper were pasted, one over another, on wood or metal 'cores'. When a sufficient thickness had been obtained, the core was removed. The resulting slab was strong, versatile and hardwearing and could be used to make all kinds of things besides being ideal for japan work. Paper work, as it was called, quickly developed into an industry which was to survive for just over 100 years. In Victorian England, papier mâché was still being used to make decorative furniture, fire screens, small tables, chairs and clock cases. Unfortunately, the craft had completely died out by the 1920's.

A new beginning

Now, at the end of the 20th century, papier mâché is enjoying a revival as a recycling craft. The old techniques of working paper and paste into a useful fabric are updated with modern adhesives. Quick-drying and easy-to-use acrylic paints make the final decoration easy to do.

Two basic techniques

There are two basic techniques in this book. The first, layering, involves pasting pieces of paper over a mould to form a shell and then the mould is removed. This technique is used to make the bowls and the Easter hen in Chapter two. Layering is also used to to cover a permanent structure or framework which is afterwards decorated. The Noah's ark and animals in the Child's play chapter and the black and white cat and sitting duck in Just for fun are examples of this technique.

The other basic technique uses paper pulp. Pulp is used to cover a basic structure, such as cardboard and is also used for modelling. The man-in-the-moon and the snowman in the Party time chapter are both examples of this technique.

For papier mâché layering, I used mixed wallpaper paste. However, this has a fungicide in it and you may not want to let your children work with the product. So, I have also provided a good recipe for making flour and water paste. If you prefer, a ready-made water-soluble paste is available from crafts shops.

Some of the ideas in this book are true recycling projects because I have used throw-away materials to make something useful or decorative. Brown paper bags and newspaper-stuffed plastic shopping bags have been transformed into toy bears, cats and ducks. Pulp egg cartons make a set of pretty egg-cups. The sea waves at the bottom of the sun mirror are made from strips cut from a fruit packing tray. The thin cardboard of cereal packets has been used for a number of structures and I found that cartons discarded by supermarkets provided me with corrugated card and a strong, rigid cardboard.

Both my young family and I have had a lot of fun in producing this book. I hope that you will enjoy making the things as much as I had in designing them. In no time at all, you will be developing the craft in your own way and go on to create even more exciting and beautiful things from just paper, card and paste.

ONE

Child's Play

Noah's ark

Let it rain – old Noah and his family, and the animals, will be safe from the deluge in this smart ark. The one pictured measures approximately 22in (56cm) long by 10in (25cm) wide.

Materials
Sheet of flexible card
Square or rectangular box for the cabin
Corrugated card
Adhesive tape
Masking tape
Clear, quick-drying glue
PVA adhesive

Brown parcel paper
White emulsion paint
Brown wax crayon
Acrylic paints

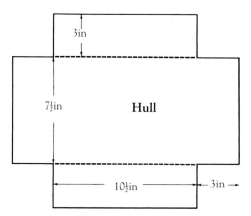

Draw the main hull on cardboard.

Cut the cardboard box for the cabin.

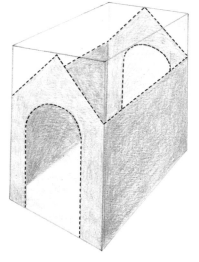

Preparation

1 Draw the main hull shape on cardboard. Score along the dotted lines and fold.

2 Cut the cardboard box to shape so that it has gable ends and a doorway.

3 Cut 2 ark sides from doubled corrugated cardboard.

4 Tape the ark sides to the hull, then bend up the ends of the deck to fit inside the hull.

Cut 2 ark sides from doubled corrugated card.

11

5 Tape across the underside of the prow and stern.

6 Glue the cabin inside the hull.

7 Cover the entire ark inside and out with pasted strips of newspaper. Leave to dry.

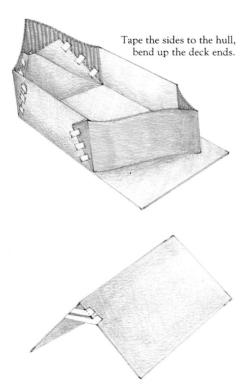

Tape the sides to the hull, bend up the deck ends.

Tape across the roof ends to hold the shape.

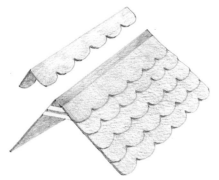

Cut scallops on one edge of the card strips.
Cut scallops on both edges of the roof ridge.
Stick the tiles to the roof, overlapping each strip.

8 Apply 3 more layers. Gently pull the sides of the ark outwards to a bow shape while the papier mâché is still damp.

9 When the hull has been shaped and the work is dry, apply 2 more layers of newspaper strips.

Roof
10 Cut a piece of card and score it down the middle so that it fits the cabin roof. Fold the roof and then tape across the ends to hold the shape.

11 From thick card, cut 10 strips to the length of the roof and 1½in (4cm) deep. Cut the ridge to the same width and twice the depth. Score down the middle of the ridge and fold.

12 Mark and cut scallops along one edge of the strips and on both edges of the ridge piece.

13 Starting at the lower edge of the roof, glue scalloped tiles to the roof sides, overlapping each strip a little. Finally, glue the ridge piece in position.

14 Cover the underside of the roof with 2–3 layers of pasted newspaper strips. Leave to dry.

15 Cover the top side of the roof with 3 layers of pasted tissue paper, pressing the tissue down between the scallops. Leave to dry. The roof remains free of the cabin so that the animals can be put in and taken out easily.

Finishing
16 Tear long strips of brown paper and glue inside the hull for the deck. Mark the plank lines with wax crayon.

17 Paint the ark as in the picture, or in colours of your choice. The window effect on the cabin wall can be painted on or you can cut rectangles of plain, coloured paper and paste them in a window arrangement.

Mr and Mrs Noah and the animals

The basic animal shapes given can be adapted to all kinds of animals. The smaller structure will make dogs and sheep. The larger structure could be adapted to make lions, tigers, zebras etc.

Materials

Plastic coated wire
Kitchen paper roll
Wallpaper paste, mixed thickly
Small pieces of cardboard
PVA adhesive
White emulsion paint
Acrylic paints

Preparation

1 Working from the outlines, bend and twist wire into animal and human shapes. It does not matter how large you make the figures as long as they fit into your ark. The human figure stands 9in (22.5cm) tall, while the zebra is 8in long and 6in tall (20 × 15cm).

Working the design

2 Tear long strips of kitchen paper and spread paste on one side. Wrap the wire structures with pasted strips, leave to dry.

3 Apply a second layer, building up the thicker places – heads, bodies etc. Add more strips as desired until you are satisfied with the shape.

4 Leave the animals and figures to dry then paint with PVA adhesive.

5 Cut ears and tails from card. Stick to the animals.

6 Paint the animals and figures with white emulsion paint.

7 Decorate the animals with acrylic paints.

Dressing the figures

8 Wrap the figures in kitchen paper and stick the overlaps to fasten. Paint the clothes (see picture) then the faces.

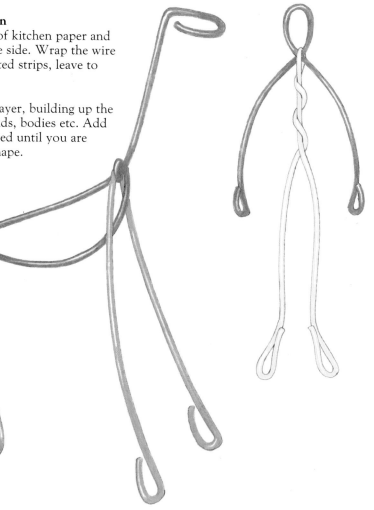

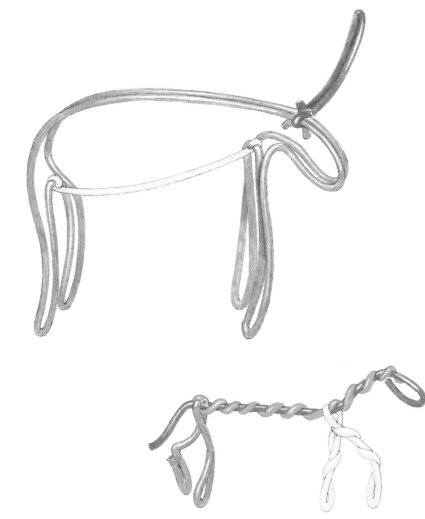

Bend wire to make the human and animals shapes.
Wrap the wire structure with pasted strips,
building up the head and body.

Sheep mobile

Hang this amusing mobile in the bedroom and the children can literally count sheep. The effect of the sheep's woolly coats is made with paper pulp applied over card shapes.

Materials
Cardboard
3–4 cups of paper pulp (refer to Better Techniques)
6 large jump rings
Acrylic paints
Wire lampshade ring, approximately 8in (20cm) diameter
Masking tape
Tissue paper
PVA adhesive
Nylon thread; brass curtain ring

Preparation
1 Trace the sheep shape. Cut 8 sheep from card.

Working the design
2 Smear paper pulp over the sheep, leaving the face area and feet. Leave to dry then turn over and do the other side of the sheep.

3 Build up the body thickness with 2 more layers of pulp, leaving each to dry between applications. Work both sides of the sheep in the same way, but always leaving the face and feet untreated.

4 Pierce a hole in the back of the sheep. Slip a jump ring through.

5 Paint the sheep fleece white and the feet and face black. Paint in the eyes.

6 Cover the wire ring with masking tape.

7 Wrap the ring with pasted tissue until the wire is thickened and smooth.

8 Trace the cloud pattern. Measure the circumference of the ring and cut a 1in

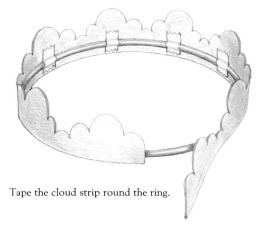
Tape the cloud strip round the ring.

(2.5cm) wide strip of card to the measurement plus 1in (2.5cm) for overlap.

9 Trace the cloud motif along the strip. Cut out.

10 Tape the cloud strip to the outside of the ring then paste tissue over the join. Cover the cloud strip with pasted tissue. Apply 2–3 layers.

11 Pierce 8 equidistant holes round the cloud edge.

12 Cut 4 lengths of thread. Tape one end to the inside of the cloud, spacing the 4 threads equidistantly. Knot the 4 ends and tie to a curtain ring.

13 Hang the clouds ring so that you can work on it. Pass threads through the 8 holes and knot. Thread the other end through the sheep's jump rings and knot.

14 Hang the sheep at alternate heights, one high, one low.

16

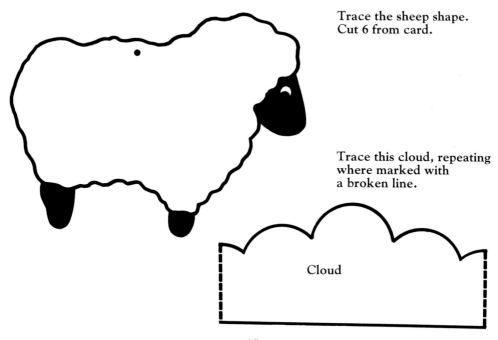

Trace the sheep shape.
Cut 6 from card.

Trace this cloud, repeating
where marked with
a broken line.

Cloud

17

Fairy doll

This little toy is almost literally made from nothing at all – just icecream sticks, a cardboard tube and a pingpong ball – plus some clever papier mâché.

Materials

Cardboard tube, 3½in (8cm) long and 2in (5cm) in diameter
4 wooden icecream sticks (or flat pieces of wood, 4½ × ½in (11 × 1cm)
4 small beads; silver wire
White emulsion paint
PVA adhesive; tissue paper; acrylic paints
Knitting yarns; small bead
White satin fabric
White net
Cocktail stick
Paper star

Preparation

1 Pierce holes at each side of the cardboard tube ⅛in (3mm) from the top edge for the arm fixtures.

2 Pierce holes to align ⅛in (3mm) from the bottom edge for fixing the legs.

3 Cut two of the sticks in half for the arms.

4 Pierce holes at the cut ends of both arm pieces.

5 Pierce holes at one end of the remaining sticks for legs.

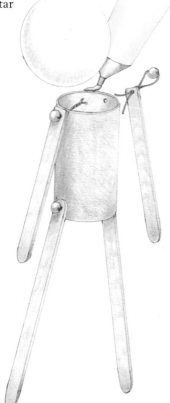

Pierce holes at the sides, top and bottom. Wire on the limbs, stick on the head.

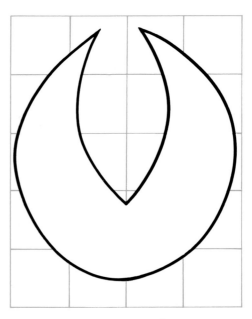

Draw this wing pattern on squared paper, scale 1 sq = 1in (2.5cm).

6 Assembly: Cut four 2in (5cm) lengths of wire. Slip a bead on a wire, pass the end through a limb then through a hole in the tube. Twist the wire ends. Work all four limbs in the same way.

7 Glue the ball head on the top of the tube using quick-drying glue.

8 Draw the wings shape and cut from thin card. Stick the wings to the back of the tube body and paint silver.

9 Wrap the arms and legs with long, pasted strips of tissue paper. When dry, apply a second layer.

10 Cover the doll's body, head and neck with pasted scraps of tissue paper. Leave to dry then apply 2 more layers.

11 Paint the entire doll with emulsion paint.

12 Paint the doll's features. Cut lengths of mixed yarns and glue across the head.

13 Cut a 12in (30cm) square each of white satin and net. Fold the squares, wrong sides facing. Gather and sew the satin round the doll's waist. Gather and sew the net skirt on top. Cut a net strip and tie round the waist. Make a net bow and stick to the forehead. Stick on a bead.

14 Paint the cocktail stick, fix the paper star to the end and stick the wand to the doll's hand.

Punch and Judy

These puppets have been favourites with generations of children. Although today's children are sometimes more sophisticated, the magic of a Punch and Judy show is as strong as ever.

Materials
Newspaper
Garden sticks, dowel rods etc,
  approximately 8in (20cm) long (one for
  each puppet)
Paper pulp mixed with PVA adhesive
  ($\frac{2}{3}$ pulp to $\frac{1}{3}$ adhesive) (refer to Better
  Techniques for making pulp)
Mixed wallpaper paste
Tissue paper
Cardboard
Acrylic paints
18in (45cm) gathered lace edging
$\frac{1}{4}$in (6mm)-wide red satin ribbon
6in (15cm) of $\frac{1}{4}$in (6mm)-wide white satin
  ribbon
12in (30cm) of $\frac{1}{4}$in (6mm)-wide white satin
  ribbon
3 bells
Blue fabric, 24in (60cm) square
Wide-striped cotton fabric 24in (60cm)
  square
Narrow-striped fabric, 12 × 4in
  (30 × 10cm)
White fabric 12 × 4in (30 × 10cm)
36in (90cm) of navy ricrac braid
White cotton fabric, 12in (30cm) square
Flat icecream stick

Preparation
1 Crumple newspaper into an oval
shape, about 4in (10cm) by 3in (7.5cm)
across for the head. Push a stick into the
underside of the head. Tape the head to
hold the shape. Tape round the bottom
of the head and on to the stick to make a
neck. Tape down the stick. Make two
heads in the same way for Punch and
Judy.

2 Trace hand shapes for both puppets.
Cut from card.

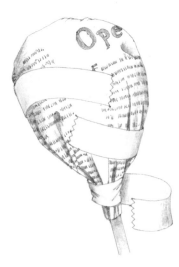

Tape the newspaper head to the stick.

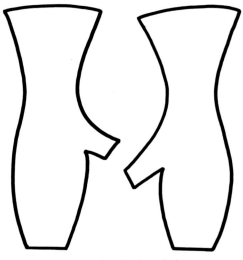

Trace left and right hand shapes.

Working the design
3 Stand the stick in a container that will
hold the head steady while you model the
features.

20

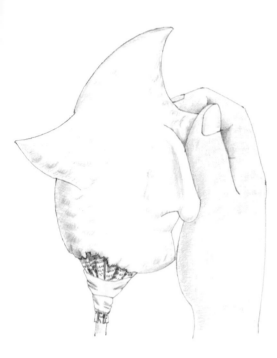

Mould pulp on to the head to get the basic features.

Trace this brim for Judy's cap.

4 Using your fingers, mould pulp on to the heads to get the basic shape of the puppets' features. Punch has a large nose and chin and a three-pointed cap on his head. Judy has a neater, pointed nose and chin. Do not work too quickly. Do the modelling over several sessions, leaving each application of pulp to dry out thoroughly.

5 When the faces are modelled, apply 3 layers of pasted tissue over the faces and down the sticks.

6 Trace the pattern and cut Judy's scalloped cap front from card. Cover the cap front with pasted tissue on both sides. Leave to dry and apply 2 more layers. Paint the cap front white.

7 Glue the cap front round Judy's head.

8 Faces and hands: Paint the puppets' heads pale pink. **Punch:** Paint a black outline round the face for the cap edge and paint the three-pointed cap black. Paint a red mask and a red mouth. Paint white eye patches with black crosses for the eyes. **Judy:** Paint black dots for eyes. Paint dark pink cheeks. Brush in brown eyebrows and a curl on the forehead. Give Judy a wide, red, smile.

9 Brush a coat of diluted PVA over both puppet heads. Build up one side of the hands with pulp. Leave to dry then cover the hands with pasted tissue. Leave to dry then apply another layer of tissue. Paint the hands pink.

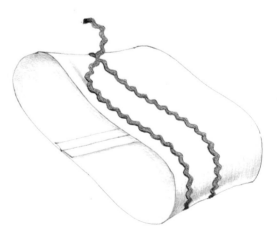

Join the ruffle ends and stick ricrac braid round the middle and near the edge.

22

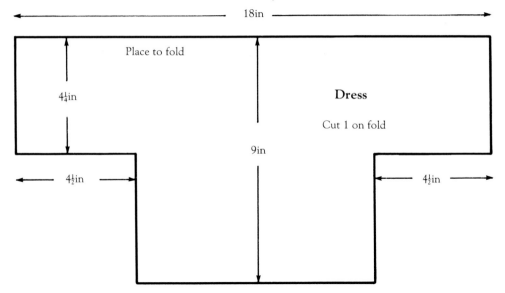

18in

Place to fold

4¼in

Dress

Cut 1 on fold

9in

4½in

4½in

Draw a pattern for both puppets' dresses from this diagram.

Dressing the puppets

10 Judy: Stick gathered lace edging round the head, behind the cap front. Tie a small red ribbon bow and stick to the top of the head.

11 From the diagram, cut Judy's dress in the wide-striped fabric. Snip a neck hole.

12 Neaten the sleeve ends. Stitch the side and underarm seams in one.

13 Turn and stitch the hem. Turn a narrow hem on the sleeve ends. Slip in the hands and gather the sleeves tightly to hold the hands.

14 Slip the dress on to the puppet stick. Stick the neckline to the stick.

15 Ruffle: Join the short ends of the ruffle fabric. Stick the ricrac braid round, just above the middle and 1¼in (3cm) away.

16 Fold the ruffle along the middle wrong sides facing and gather both raw edges together. Slip over the puppet's head and pull up the gathers tightly. Knot the thread ends to secure.

17 Punch: Make a dark blue garment in the same way as Judy's dress. Insert the hands as for Judy.

18 Make a ruffle as for Judy's but without the ricrac braid decoration. Slip on to the puppet.

19 Pierce the points of Punch's cap. Thread fine wire through and slip on the bells.

Punch's stick
20 Tear small pieces of kitchen roll paper and paste round an icecream stick, so that it is thicker at one end. Finish with 2 layers of pasted tissue.

21 When dry, paint the stick white. Tie a red ribbon bow round the base of the stick. Stick to Punch's hand with PVA adhesive.

Judy's baby

Materials
Tin foil
Newspaper
Mixed wallpaper paste
Tissue paper
Acrylic paints
Piece of white cotton fabric 8in (20cm) square
6in (15cm) piece of pre-gathered lace

Preparation
1 Crumple tin foil into a 1½in (3cm)-diameter ball. Crumple more tinfoil into a 3 × 1in (7.5 × 2.5cm) sausage shape.

Working the design
2 Tape the ball and sausage shape together. Tear newspaper into small strips and paste all over the figure. Leave to dry. Apply 2 more layers of pasted newspaper strips.

3 Paste two layers of tissue paper over the ball head.

4 Paint the face pink.

5 Lay the baby figure on the square of white fabric. Wrap the baby and stick the fabric in place.

6 Stick gathered lace edging round the face.

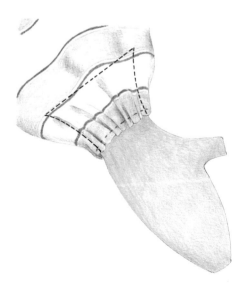

Gather the sleeves round the hand and pull up the gathers tightly.

Tape the ball and sausage shapes together.

Mushroom savings bank

What fun to have a money box that looks as though it came out of a fairy story! The mushroom makes a perfect gift for children – and perhaps it will encourage them to save.

Materials
A bowl, about 7in (18cm) diameter
Petroleum jelly
2 cups of mixed paper pulp (refer to
    Better Techniques)
Cardboard tube, about 3in (7.5cm)
    diameter, 4in (10cm) long
Thin cardboard
Kitchen paper roll
Tissue paper
Mixed wallpaper paste
Adhesive tape
Masking tape
White emulsion paint
Acrylic paints
PVA adhesive

Preparation
1 Grease the inside of the bowl.

Working the design
2 Spread pulp on the bottom of the bowl and about halfway up the sides. Try and keep the top edge even. Leave to dry.

3 When dry, fill in any cracks with more pulp. Even up the edges with pulp. Leave to dry again then remove the shell from the mould carefully.

Working the design
4 Cut a circle of card to fit the bottom of the tube. Tape in place

5 Take 3 sheets of kitchen paper, fold in four then tape round the sealed end of the tube.

6 Cover the tube and base with a layer of pasted tissue paper. Leave until dry. Apply 2 more layers, leaving the work to dry between each application.

7 Using a sharp crafts knife, cut a money slit across the middle of the mushroom cap.

8 Measure the depth of the mushroom cap. Cut a strip of card to this depth by the circumference of the tube plus $\frac{1}{2}$in (1cm). Overlap the strip ends and tape to form a collar.

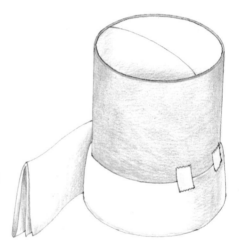

Tape folded kitchen paper round the bottom of the tube to thicken the base.

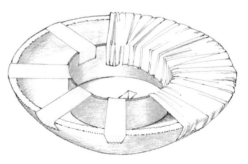

Hold the inside collar in place with masking tape strips, cover with creased, pasted tissue paper.

9 Tape the card collar in the middle of the inside mushroom cap.

10 Using masking tape, fix strips from the inside of the collar to the outside of the mushroom cap.

11 Cover the tapes with pasted strips of tissue paper. Crease the strips as you apply them so that they look like the gills of a mushroom.

12 Paint the finished mushroom and cap with acrylic colours. Give a final coat of diluted PVA adhesive.

Toad Hall
To vary the design, paint a blue door and 2 windows on the mushroom stalk. Paint a bell pull on the right and some small flowers round the bottom of the mushroom.

TWO

Paper the House

❧

Sun mirror

This magical-looking mirror is decorated with the sun, stars and clouds above and waves and starfish below. It is sure to have pride of place in your home.

Materials
8in (20cm) square mirror
10in (25cm) square of hardboard
4 sticky pads
Corrugated cardboard
Brown paper tape
Thick stem wire, 8in (20cm) long
Clear, adhesive tape
PVA adhesive
12 cocktail sticks
Thin cardboard
Pulp cardboard fruit packing (refer to Better Techniques)
Mixed paper pulp (refer to Better Techniques)
Mixed wallpaper paste
Tissue paper
Clear, quick-drying adhesive
White emulsion paint
Gold paint
Bronze-coloured cream paint (Treasure gold)

Preparation
1 Fasten the mirror to the hardboard with sticky pads.

2 Cut 2 pieces of corrugated card 6 × 1½in (15 × 3cm).

3 Fix them to the sides of the mirror with strips of brown paper tape.

4 Bend the stem wire into a semi-circle. Tape it to the centre top of the hardboard.

5 Moisten pieces of brown paper tape and cover the wire.

6 Cut 2 strips from the pulp cardboard fruit packing. Stick one overlapping the other across the bottom of the mirror for waves. The strips should overlap the bottom edges of the side pillars.

7 Cut pieces of card with scalloped 'cloud' edges. Stick the clouds round the top of the mirror, overlapping some on to the mirror edges. Cut another cloud-edged strip and stick it down the right-hand edge of the mirror, overlapping on to the glass.

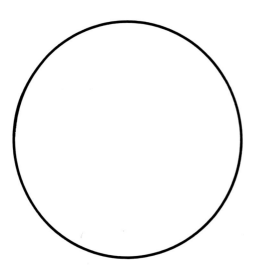

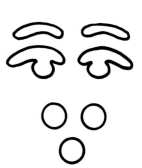

Trace these shapes to decorate the mirror.

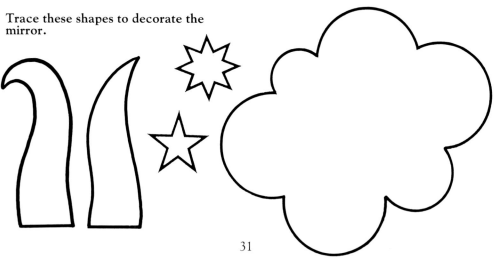

31

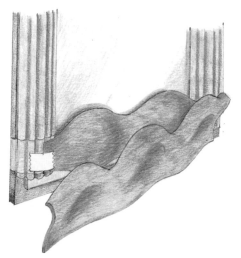

Cut strips from fruit packing. Stick strips overlapping for waves.

Overlap cloud shapes on to the mirror edges.

Working the design

8 Paste torn pieces of newspaper across the wired semi-circle. Apply more pasted pieces across the hardboard and mirror edges and across the straight edges of the cloud strips.

9 Paste pieces of tissue across the clouds, the sun's semi-circle backing and the waves. When the first layer is dry, apply 2–3 more layers, allowing the pasted tissue to crumple as you work.

10 Trace the patterns. From thin card, cut 2 pillar tops, 2 eyes and eyebrows for the sun, 2 cheeks, a nose and a chin. Cut 3 eight-pointed stars. Cut 2 five-pointed stars.

11 Trace the 2 sun ray patterns. Cut 6 of each from thin card. Cut a 2¼in (6cm)-diameter circle of card for the sun's face.

12 Glue the cocktail sticks to the wire across the semi-circle and on to the top of the mirror.

13 Glue the sun rays on to the cocktail sticks, alternating the shapes.

14 Build up the thickness of the sun rays with pulp. When dry, wrap the rays with pasted tissue.

15 Stick the sun's face over the rays. Build up the surface with pulp. When dry, paste tissue over the edges of the circle.

Finishing

16 Stick the features on the sun's face. Stick the eight-point stars to the clouds. Stick the tops of the pillars in place. Stick the five-point star starfish below the waves. Paste tissue over everything.

17 Paste tissue over the pillar tops and pillars.

18 If there are spaces in your design that appear to need filling, paste pieces of pasted kitchen roll paper down for cloud effects.

19 Paint the finished piece with white emulsion paint. When it is dry, paint gold. Finally, finger-dab over the gold with bronze.

20 Apply 2–3 layers of pasted, torn newspaper strips to the back of the mirror. When the papier mâché is completely dry, paint the surface gold.

Smiling sun

Simply made on a cardboard base, this wall plaque looks solid and metallic when finished with a coat of gold paint. It makes an ideal decoration for a dark corner or a hallway.

Materials

Thick cardboard
Clear, quick-drying glue
Thin, flexible cardboard
Cocktail sticks
Mixed paper pulp (refer to Better
   Techniques)
Kitchen paper roll
Mixed wallpaper paste
Gold paint
Black paint

Preparation

1 Cut 2 circles of thick card, 6½in and
5½in diameter (16 and 13cm diameter).

2 Using a large coin as a template, cut 10
circles of kitchen paper. Put aside.

3 Mark the larger card circle into
quarters, then make 2 equidistant marks
in each quarter segment.

4 Glue cocktail sticks at each mark so
that they protrude over the edge of the
card about three-quarters of their length.

5 Trace the sun ray shapes. Transfer to
thin card and cut 6 of each shape.

6 Alternating shapes, tape them to the
cocktail sticks.

7 Glue the smaller card circle to cover
the ends of the cocktail sticks. Leave to
dry.

Working the design

8 Using 1 cup of mixed paper pulp,
spread a thin layer all over the sun. Leave
to dry. If cracks appear, fill them with
more pulp and leave to dry.

9 Model the face with pulp and then
with small pieces of pasted newspaper.

10 Build up the sun rays with pulp, then
with pasted newspaper strips.

11 Paste 5 paper circles, one on another,
on each side of the sun's face for cheeks.

12 When the work is completely dry,
paint the sun with 2 coats of white
emulsion paint.

13 Paint the sun gold then, when dry,
rub black paint into the folds and
crevices using a scrap of fabric.

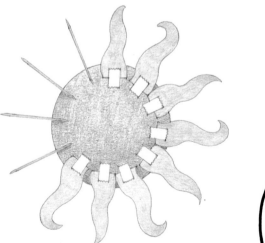

Alternating shapes, tape the rays to the cocktail
sticks.

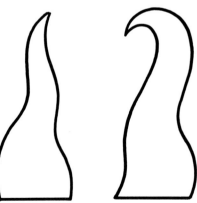

Trace these sun rays.

Easter hen

Make this colourful hen and bowl for your Easter breakfast table. Crumple a yellow paper serviette in the bowl and arrange the breakfast eggs in the 'nest'.

Materials
An inflated round balloon
Newspaper torn into small pieces
Tissue paper
Mixed wallpaper paste
PVA adhesive
Kitchen roll paper
Acrylic paints

Preparation
1 Set the balloon in a cereal bowl to keep it steady while you work.

Working the design
2 Dampen pieces of torn newspaper and apply to the surface of the balloon. Leave to dry, then apply pasted pieces of newspaper over the balloon.

3 When dry, apply a second layer of pasted newspaper. Leave to dry then apply 4–5 more layers, leaving the work to dry between each layer.

4 Pop the balloon and remove it from the paper shell. Trim the shell edges.

5 Trace the head and tail patterns. Cut from card. Fix in place on the paper shell with pieces of sticky tape.

6 Crumple little pads of tissue and tape them on either side of the head and tail to build them up.

7 Paste small pieces of kitchen roll paper over the tissue pads to smooth out the surface.

8 Paste 2 layers of tissue paper all over the hen to smooth off the surface.

Bowl
9 Smear petroleum jelly round the inside of a bowl a little bigger than the circumference of the hen body.

10 Cover the inside of the bowl with pasted newspaper strips. Leave to dry, then repeat the process 3–4 times. When completely dry, twist the paper shell and lift from the bowl.

11 Trim the edge of the bowl into scallops.

12 Cut a strip of card ¾in (18mm) deep by 20in (50cm). Tape the ends to make a circle. Tape the circle to the underside of the bowl for a standing rim.

13 Paste tissue all over the outside of the bowl and over the edges of the standing rim. Leave to dry, then apply 2 more layers.

14 Paste tissue to the inside of the bowl in the same way. Build up the inside of the bowl until the hen lid sits neatly in the bowl.

15 Tear narrow strips of tissue and paste them over the scalloped edge.

16 Paint the hen and bowl, inside and out, with white emulsion paint.

17 Paint the bowl red with a black trim. Paint the hen, following the picture.

18 Varnish the finished hen and bowl on the outside or coat with diluted PVA adhesive.

Tape the head to the body, tape crumpled tissue each side of the head.

Tape the strip ends, then tape the ring under the bowl for a rim.

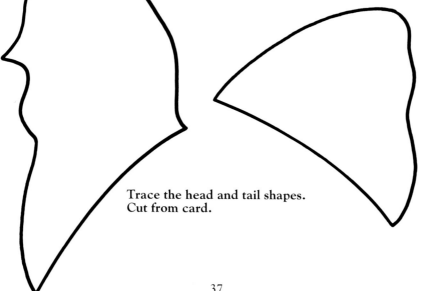

Trace the head and tail shapes. Cut from card.

37

Egg-cups

Children will love making their own breakfast egg-cups from egg trays and they can decorate them in any way they like. Why not make one for each member of the family for Easter?

Materials
Pulp paper egg tray
PVA adhesive
Clear, sticky tape
Tissue paper
Flour and water paste (refer to Better
  Techniques)
White emulsion paint
Acrylic paints
Clear, polyurethane varnish

Preparation
1 Cut sections from the egg tray as large as possible. There will be gaps where the sections adjoin. These are filled with tape later.

2 Cut more sections and trim these down to approximately ⅝in (15mm) deep. These are for the egg-cup bases.

3 Stick the egg-cups to bases. If there are gaps in the edges of the cup or base, tape across the gaps.

Tape over any gaps in the sections. Stick the egg-cup to the base piece.

Candle holders
Egg carton segments make pretty candle holders for party tables. Stick trimmed segments to squares of thick card. Cut 4 petals from carton pieces, tape to the cup edges. Paste over 5–6 layers of tissue. Paint and varnish.

Working the design
4 Cover the entire egg-cup with pieces of pasted tissue. Leave to dry out then repeat the process 6 more times, leaving each layer to dry before applying the next.

5 When dry, paint the egg-cups with white emulsion paint. Decorate with acrylic colours. Varnish inside and out.

Decorating egg-cups
Painted egg-cups make acceptable gifts and can be presented at Easter, complete with a fresh egg or a chocolate egg. If you cannot draw, decorate egg-cups with stencilled designs – there are many small, suitable stencil motifs to be found in crafts shops. Alternatively, cut motifs from coloured magazine pages and paste them to the egg-cup. Varnish over the decoration several times until the edges of the cut-outs can no longer be felt with a finger nail. Rub-down letters can also be used to make initials or words.

Rose bowl

The paper pulp method is used to make this bowl and the secret of success lies in ensuring that the pulp is applied inside the bowl evenly and smoothly.

Bowl for a mould
Petroleum jelly
4 cups of mixed paper pulp (refer to
    Better Techniques)
Fine sandpaper
Acrylic paints
PVA adhesive
Clear polyurethane varnish

Preparation
1 Grease the inside of the bowl with petroleum jelly.

Working the design
2 Press an even layer of pulp, ¼in (6mm) thick, to the inside of the bowl. Begin at the bottom of the bowl and work up the sides. Leave to dry.

3 If cracks appear after drying, fill them with more pulp and smooth out the surface. Leave to dry again.

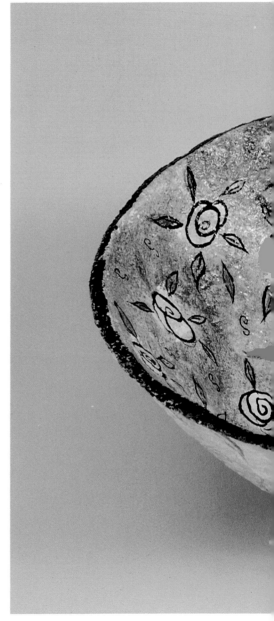

Press an even layer of pulp inside the bowl.

4 Twist the pulp bowl gently to remove it from the mould.

5 If there are uneven places on the edges, fill out with paper pulp. Leave to dry.

6 Rub the edges of the bowl with sandpaper for a smooth finish.

7 Paint the bowl inside and out in a plain colour or in a decorative pattern, such as the simple rose design in the picture.

8 Give the finished bowl 2 coats of diluted PVA adhesive or 4–5 coats of polyurethane varnish. Leave each coat to dry before applying the next.

Scalloped bowl

In this project, the bowl is shaped over a round balloon which is popped after the papier mâché has dried. The edges of the bowl are then cut into scallops but they can be left straight if you prefer.

Materials
Round balloon, inflated
Newspaper torn into small pieces
Tissue paper
Kitchen paper roll
Wallpaper paste, mixed thickly
PVA adhesive
Giftwrap paper
Gold modeller's paint

Preparation
1 Place the inflated balloon in a suitable container to support it while you work.

Working the design
2 Paste small pieces of newspaper and apply them to the surface of the ballon, overlapping the edges slightly. Cover just over half of the balloon's surface.

3 When the first layer is dry, apply another layer and leave to dry.

4 Apply 3 more layers in the same way.

5 Prick the balloon to deflate it and gently pull it away from the papier mâché.

6 Use a small lid to mark scallops round the edge of the bowl. Cut with sharp scissors.

7 Using newspaper and kitchen paper alternately, paste layers of strips over the inside and outside of the bowl until a thickness has been built up. Take care that you keep the shape of the scalloped edges. You will find that narrow strips of paper work best here. Leave the work to dry out between each layer.

Mark scallops round the bowl.

Use narrow strips of paper over the scalloped edge.

42

8 Apply a final layer of pasted tissue to give a smooth finish, inside and out.

Decorating the bowl
9 Tear pieces of giftwrap and paste over the outside of the bowl, overlapping pieces for an attractive effect. Alternatively, if the giftwrap design is suitable, cut motifs from the paper and apply these to the bowl, overlapping them so that the surface is covered.

10 When the bowl is dry, brush on a coat of diluted PVA adhesive inside and out. Leave to dry.

11 Paint the scalloped edge with gold paint.

12 If you prefer, coat the bowl with white emulsion paint then decorate with a painted design.

Bowl of cherries

Display lots of these luscious-looking cherries in a papier mâché bowl for a pretty ornament. The bowl can be made with either the paper pulp or layered paper methods.

Materials
Black (annealed) stem wires
Mixed paper pulp (refer to Better
    Techniques)
White paper
Acrylic paints
PVA adhesive

Preparation
1 Cut the stem wire to 2½in (6cm) long for double cherry stems and to 1¼in (3cm) for single cherries. Bend the longer wires in half.

Working the design
2 Mould small cherry-sized balls and press them on to the wire ends. Leave to dry, filling any cracks as they appear.

3 **Leaves:** Cut rectangles of paper, 1½ × ¾in (4 × 2cm). Paste 2 rectangles of paper together with a stem wire between,

leaving a long end protruding. Leave to dry, then paint green on both sides.

4 Give the leaves a coat of diluted PVA adhesive on the top side only and leave to dry.

5 Cut the leaves to shape.

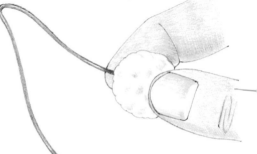

Mould cherry-sized balls from pulp and press on to the wire ends.

Paste wire between 2 paper rectangles. Paint the paper green, cut out leaf shapes.

Small fruit bowl
Set a small bowl (like a cereal bowl) upside-down on a flat surface. Dip strips of torn newspaper in water and apply all over the bowl. When the strips are almost dry, apply 5–6 layers of pasted strips then 2 layers of pasted tissue. Lift the finished bowl from the mould, trim the edges then finish with narrow strips of pasted tissue. Paint with emulsion paint and decorate.

Alternatively, make the bowl by greasing the inside with petroleum jelly and press paper pulp to the bottom and sides.

6 Paint the cherries and the stems. Give the cherries only a coat of diluted PVA adhesive for a glossy finish.

7 Fix the leaves to the fruit stems by twisting the wires together. Bend the leaf tips for a natural effect.

Tea tray

Creating this smart papier mâché tea tray could not be easier. All you need is an inexpensive plastic tray for a mould plus pasted newspaper – and some decorative giftwrap.

Materials
Metal or plastic tray
Petroleum jelly
Newspaper torn into small strips
Mixed wallpaper paste
Kitchen roll paper
Patterned giftwrap
PVA adhesive
Clear polyurethane varnish

Preparation
1 Smear petroleum jelly over the surface of the tray.

Working the design
2 Beginning at one side of the tray and working round the edges and towards the centre, paste newspaper strips to the tray. Overlap the pieces.

3 Leave the work to dry, then repeat the process 5–6 times, leaving the work to dry completely between each application.

4 Ease the paper shell from the tray.

5 Tear pieces of kitchen roll paper, paste them and apply a layer over the surface of the paper shell, over the edges and on to the back. Leave to dry.

6 Apply another layer to back and front but using newspaper strips this time.

7 Now work on the front of the tray only, applying alternate layers of newspaper and kitchen roll paper, leaving each layer to dry before working the next. Work 6–8 layers.

8 The tray should now be strong and inflexible. Add more layers if you think the tray requires strengthening.

9 When the last layer is dry, tear small pieces of giftwrap and paste them to the tray to cover the surface. When the paper is dry, other decorative motifs can be added. When the decoration is completed, brush diluted PVA over the tray.

10 Paint the back of the tray black. Give the front a final coat of polyurethane varnish.

At the end of the 18th century, Henry Clay of Birmingham, England, invented a way of making papier mâché by pasting whole sheets of paper together over a wood or metal core. Try the technique yourself to make a tray. Choose a square or rectangular metal or plastic tray. Work on a flat surface protected with plastic sheeting. Brush a large sheet of newspaper with wallpaper paste then carefully spread another sheet on top. Brush the surface with paste and place another sheet of newspaper on top. Try not to get creases in the paper. Work 12–15 layers. Leave the pasted paper to dry until it feels like a piece of leather. Grease the tray's surface. Lift the papier mâché on to the tray and press it to the tray's shape. Trim excess paper from the edges at this stage. Leave to dry slowly in a warm place. Finish the tray's edges with small strips of newspaper. Paint with emulsion and decorate.

Blue vase

This elegant ornament started as a plastic detergent bottle and 4 pipecleaners – but no one would guess its humble origins. Any plastic container with a pleasing shape can be used.

Materials
Plastic bottle
Newspaper torn into strips
Kitchen paper roll
Tissue paper
Mixed wallpaper paste
PVA adhesive
4 pipecleaners
White emulsion paint
Acrylic paints

Preparation
1 Cut the top from the plastic bottle.

Working the design
2 Paste newspaper strips all over the bottle, taking strips over the cut edge to the inside.

3 When the first layer is dry, work a second layer but this time using kitchen paper roll. Work 4–5 layers, alternating the paper each time. Leave to dry.

4 Cover the vase with a layer of pasted tissue.

5 Secure 2 pipecleaners, $\frac{1}{2}$in (1cm) apart with strips of tape, positioning them just below the top edge of the vase. Bend the pipecleaners into shape then secure the ends to the vase with tape. Do the same on the opposite side of the vase.

6 Wrap the pipecleaner handles with strips of pasted tissue, keeping the pipecleaners $\frac{1}{2}$in (1cm) apart and the curves true.

7 Apply 3 layers of pasted tissue all over the vase and leave to dry out.

8 Paint the vase inside (as far as possible) and outside with white emulsion paint.

9 Decorate with acrylic colours.

If the vase is to be used for fresh flowers in water, varnish both inside and out. Give 4–5 coats, leaving each coat to dry before applying the next.

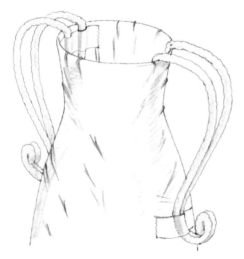

Bend 2 pipecleaners to shape and tape to vase side.

Seashore frame

Here's a way to make good use of shells collected while on holiday. The basic idea could be adapted for a large, kitchen pinboard, or for a box top. Small pearl beads could be added for contrast.

Materials
Frame cut from hardboard
Smaller ready-made picture frame
Modelling clay or mixed paper pulp
Clear adhesive
Shells
Twine, or smooth parcel string
Mixed wallpaper paste
Tissue paper
White emulsion paint
Acrylic paints

Preparation
1 Stick the hardboard frame to the picture frame.

2 Mould a starfish from modelling clay, or cut a cardboard starfish shape and build up the surface with paper pulp.

3 Stick the starfish at bottom left of the frame.

4 Stick the shells centre top and bottom right of the frame.

5 Using the glue nozzle, mark thin lines of adhesive on the frame where the string is to be.

6 Lay the string along the glue lines and lightly press down.

Working the design
7 When the adhesive is completely dry, brush paste over the entire frame. Brush pieces of tissue on to the frame so that the shells, starfish and string show in relief.

8 Paste the tissue edges over to the back of the frame. Add 2 more layers in the same way, making sure that the tissue edges are taken over to the back so that the frame edges are rounded off.

9 You may find that the starfish needs more layers of tissue.

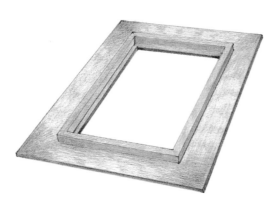

Stick the hardboard frame to the picture frame.

Mark lines of adhesive for the string patterns.

10 When the pasted tissue is dry, give the frame 2 coats of white emulsion paint. Leave to dry.

11 Paint the frame pale blue and the starfish yellow. Brush yellow over the shells and along the string lines.

51

Art Deco plate

Papier mâché plates are strong and long-lasting and are ideal for displaying on a dresser or on the wall. They can safely be used for dry foods, fruit or sweets but should not be put into water.

Materials
Plate for a mould
Petroleum jelly
Newspaper torn into $4 \times \frac{1}{2}$in (10×1cm) strips
Mixed wallpaper paste
Tissue paper
PVA adhesive
White emulsion paint
Acrylic paints

Preparation
1 Smear the surface and edges of the plate with petroleum jelly.

Working the design
2 Brush paste on to one side of the paper strips. Apply to the plate. Start at the edges and work towards the centre, overlapping the strips.

3 When the plate has a complete layer of paper, leave to dry.

4 Apply 5 more layers, leaving the work to dry between each application.

5 After the final layer, gently lift the paper shell from the plate. Trim the edges with sharp scissors.

6 Paste small pieces of tissue paper over the surface of the shell, taking the tissue over the edges. Then work the back of the shell.

7 Continue adding layers of pasted tissue paper until the paper plate feels thick and solid and the surface is smooth.

8 When the plate is completely dry, paint it with white emulsion paint.

9 Finally, decorate the plate with acrylic colours.

Paste newspaper strips to the plate mould, starting at the edges.

Geometric design

Measure and mark the middle of the plate. Draw lines dividing the plate into quarters. Divide the quarters making eighths. Divide the segments twice to make 32 lines radiating from the middle. Measure and mark 1in (2.5cm) in from the plate edge. Draw a line all round. Measure and mark a line ¾in (18mm) away and then a third line ½in (1cm) away. This makes a chequered border all round the plate. Paint alternate spaces black. For a different effect, paint the border in 4 or 5 bright colours, or paint a motif in each space on the white ground.

Blue printed jug

In this project, the papier mâché is worked over a long balloon and the finished jug is hand-printed with flowers. You could also cut motifs from flowered gift paper and stick them to the jug.

Materials
Inflated long balloon
Newspaper torn into small pieces
Mixed wallpaper paste
Thin card
Clear, sticky tape
Tissue paper
2 florist's stub wires
Masking tape
Acrylic paints
Plastic eraser
Sharp scalpel, crafts knife
PVA adhesive

Preparation
1 Stand the balloon in a mug to hold it steady while you work on it.

Working the design
2 Cover the top 8in (20cm) of the balloon with newspaper pieces dipped in water. Leave to dry, then repeat the process 5–6 times with pasted newspaper, leaving the work to dry between each application.

3 Pop the balloon and gently pull it from the work.

4 With a sharp knife, cut the rounded end off the paper shell. Trim the other end neatly.

5 Measure across the paper shell and cut a circle of card to fit the base. Tape the base in place and then cover the join with pasted tissue, inside and out.

6 Cut a triangular piece from the top edge of the jug. Cut a larger triangle of card, fold it and tape into the cutaway area for a pouring lip.

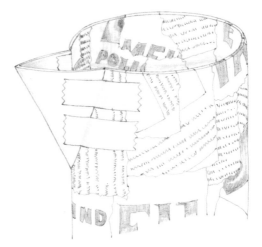
Fold a card triangle and tape in the cutaway area.

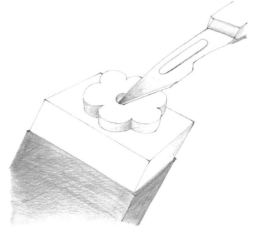
Cut the drawn motif in relief from the eraser.

7 **Handle:** Cut a strip of masking tape to the same length as the stub wires. Press the wires on to the sticky surface. Press another strip of tape on top.

8 Bend the handle to shape and tape to the side of the jug.

9 Cover the handle with strips of pasted tissue.

10 Paste 2 layers of tissue all over the jug to smooth off the surface.

Decoration
11 Paint the jug with white emulsion paint. Then paint it with cream-coloured acrylic paint.

12 Printing blocks: Using a fine, fibre-tipped pen, copy the large flower on to the flat end of the eraser. Using a scalpel knife, carefully cut around the motif so that it stands in relief.

13 Mix a little acrylic paint in a saucer. Dip in the printing block and print large flowers over the jug (see picture).

14 When the large flowers have been printed, slice the top off the eraser and copy and cut the small flower motif. Print small flowers on the jug.

15 Working in the same way, cut and print the stems and then, finally, the leaves.

16 If the design appears to need some linking stems, these can be painted in using a fine brush.

17 Paint a line round the jug rim.

18 Give the jug a final coat of diluted PVA adhesive.

Flower patterns
Choose a wallpaper printed with a small flower motif in a single colour on a white ground. Tear the wallpaper into small, circular pieces, about 1in (2.5cm) across. Paint the jug white. Paste the scraps to the jug, overlapping the edges. Varnish.

Trace these motifs for eraser block printing.

THREE

Just for Fun

Fish brooch

What a catch! Display your papier mâché fish on a brooch – it will be a talking point with your friends. This is a project older children will enjoy – they might be able to create other creatures.

Materials
Medium card
Mixed paper pulp (refer to Better
  Techniques)
Mixed wallpaper paste (or a water-based
  paper adhesive)
Tissue paper
Frosted acrylic paints
Brooch mount
Old bead necklace (or small beads and
  florist's wire)
Jump rings
Craft gem stone

Preparation
1 Trace the patterns and cut the shapes
from thin card.

Working the design
2 Build up the shapes with a little paper
pulp.

3 When the pulp is dry, paste tissue over
the shapes to smooth the surface. Work
the back of the shapes with tissue also.

Assembly
4 Paint the fish with frosted acrylic
colours. Pierce a hole at the top of each
and slip a jump ring through.

5 Glue the two wave pieces together and
paint.

6 Pierce three holes in the lower edge.
Slip jump rings through.

7 Suspend the fish on short lengths of
bead necklace and then attach to the
brooch jump rings. If beads and wire are
being used, thread the beads then attach
to the jump rings.

8 Glue the gem stone to the brooch.

Stick the wave shapes to the pin. Slip beads on to
the jump rings.

Trace these shapes and cut from card.

58

Bright bracelets

Hand-crafted bracelets look expensive and smart, especially when they are decorated to match an outfit. Two methods are described here – layering over a card ring and over wire.

RING BRACELET
Materials
Cardboard ring
Newspaper
Kitchen roll paper
Tissue paper
Mixed wallpaper paste
White emulsion paint
Acrylic paints

Preparation
1 If a ready-made card ring is not available, make a ring to the required dimensions.

Working the design
2 Paste torn strips of newspaper and wrap the ring. Leave to dry.

3 Paste torn strips of kitchen roll paper and wrap the ring. Leave to dry.

4 Continue, wrapping the ring with alternate layers of newspaper and kitchen roll strips until the edges are rounded.

5 At this stage, you can finish the bracelet with 2–3 layers of pasted tissue to smooth off the surface. Alternatively, if a rounded shape is required, build up the thickness of the bracelet by applying strips round it. Finish with strips of pasted tissue.

6 Paint the finished bracelet with white emulsion paint then decorate.

WIRE AND TAPE BRACELET
Materials
Florists' stub wires
Masking tape
Newspaper
Mixed wallpaper paste
Tissue paper
White emulsion paint
Acrylic paints

Preparation
1 Form two circlets of wire, twisting the ends together. Bind with pasted tissue until the joins cannot be seen.

2 Join the two rings to make a bracelet of the desired width using masking tape.

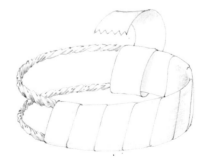

Join the two tissue-covered wire rings with strips of masking tape.

Making card rings
Using a pair of compasses, draw a circle to the desired size on thin card. Cut out the hole. Cut a strip of thin card to the depth of the bracelet. Fit it into the hole. Allow the strip to expand and fill the hole and then mark the overlap. Remove the strip and trim away the excess card. Butt the strip ends and tape the join. This method can also be used to make cardboard tubes.

Working the design

3 Cover the bracelet with small, torn, pasted newspaper pieces until the desired thickness has been built up. Finish with 2–3 layers of pasted tissue.

4 Paint the bracelet with white emulsion paint inside and out.

5 Decorate the bracelet with painted designs using acrylic paints. Alternatively, choose one of the decorating techniques described.

Ideas for decorating

● Press craft gemstones into the final layers of pasted tissue to make indentations, then stick the stones in place when the papier mâché is dry.
● Draw lines of adhesive round the painted bracelet and press thin, gold cord along the lines. Varnish over the cords afterwards.
● Crumple ovals of coloured foil, stick in place and edge them with gold cord. Give the decoration 2 coats of varnish.

Teddy bear

Three large paper bags and shredded paper make this appealing bear. Children will love him, to sit on the bedside table, but grown-up bear lovers will treasure this Teddy.

Materials
3 large paper bags approximately 8 × 8in
  (20 × 20cm)
Shredded or torn-up newspaper
Clear adhesive tape
Mixed pulp (refer to Better Techniques)
Masking tape
PVA adhesive
Toy bear eyes, or beads
Acrylic paints
18in (45cm) satin ribbon, 1in (2.5cm)
  wide

Preparation
1 Draw the leg and arm shapes on paper bags. Cut out as shown on the dotted lines.

2 Tape the cut edges of the shapes.

3 Stuff the 2 legs and 2 arms with torn-up newspaper.

4 Roll a 3in (7.5cm)-diameter ball of newspaper for the bear's head. Tape to hold the shape.

5 Stuff the remaining bag with paper for the bear's body. Use masking tape to shape the body.

6 Tape the head, arms and legs to the body.

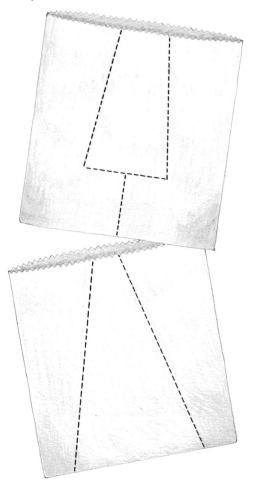

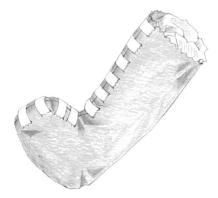

Tape the edges and stuff the leg with torn newspaper.

Draw the arms and legs on paper bags, cut out.

Working the design

7 Mix 2 cups of pulp with ¾ cup of PVA adhesive. Using a knife, spread the mixture all over the bear's body, head and limbs. Leave to dry.

8 Mix more paper pulp and PVA. Working slowly, and a little at a time, build up the shape of the head and nose. Press the eyes into the head to leave indentations. Leave the modelling to dry

between stages – do not try to do too much shaping at one time. Build up and shape the ears with blobs of pulp.

9 Stick the eyes (or beads) into the indentations.

10 Paint the bear with acrylic colours.

11 Tie a ribbon bow round the bear's neck.

Sitting duck

Decoy ducks are popular as room accessories and this papier mâché model looks very authentic. The painted decoration is important if you are to achieve the right effect.

Materials
Large plastic shopping bag
Masking tape
Newspaper
Brown paper bag approximately 8in
 (20cm) square
Tissue paper
Mixed wallpaper paste
Thin cardboard
White emulsion paint
Acrylic paints
PVA adhesive

Preparation
1 Draw the wing and tail shapes on squared paper and cut from thin card.

2 Fold up the corners of the plastic bag and tape. Stuff with crumpled newspaper. Tape the bag to form a pear shape.

3 Cut a corner from the brown paper bag. Tape the cut edges closed. Fold over the opposite corner and tape down. Stuff with tissue paper. Tape the bag to form the duck's head. Crumple pieces of tissue paper and tape to the head to assist the shaping.

4 Tape the head to the rounded end of the body.

5 Tape the wings to the sides of the body, crossing the wing tips. Tape the two tails to the end of the body, the larger tail on top.

Smooth out the body bumps with tape.

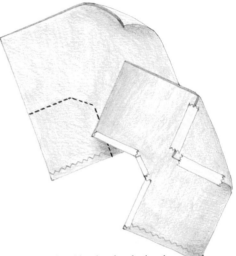

Cut a paper bag like this for the head.
Tape the edges.

Working the design
6 Tear newspaper strips and paste them all over the duck. Leave to dry.

7 Apply 3–4 layers in the same way, leaving each layer to dry before applying the next.

8 The duck should feel 'solid' at this stage. Apply more layers of newspaper strips if necessary. Paste 3 layers of tissue over the duck to smooth the surface.

9 Paint the duck with white emulsion paint.

10 Working from the picture, decorate the duck.

11 Give the duck a final coat of diluted PVA adhesive.

Tape up the corners of a shopping bag.

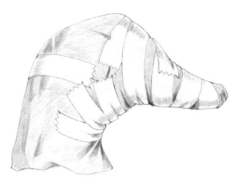

Shape the stuffed bag to a duck's head.

Draw patterns for the wings and tails.
Scale 1 sq = 1in (2.5cm).

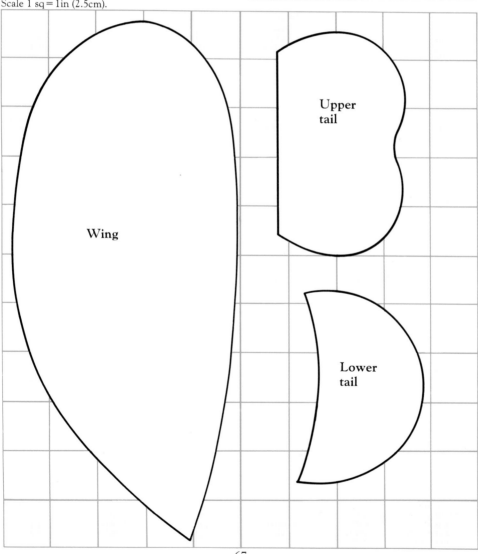

Wing

Upper
tail

Lower
tail

Sleeping cat

This dozing feline will rest by the fireside or by a chair. Although it looks complex, the cat is, in fact, very easy to make and is based on a paper bag and a plastic shopping bag.

Materials
Large, brown paper bag
Plastic shopping bags
Tissue paper
Clear, sticky tape
Thin cardboard
Newspaper
Mixed wallpaper paste
White emulsion paint
Acrylic paints
PVA adhesive

Preparation
1 Cut three corners from the paper bag and tape the edges. Stuff with the plastic bags.

2 Crumple tissue paper into a ball for the head and tape to hold the shape.

Cut the corners from a paper bag and tape.

68

3 Tape the head to the paper bag body. Crumple some more tissue and tape beside the head to round off the body so that the shape of a curled-up cat is obtained. (Refer to the picture.)

4 Trace the ear shape and cut 2 from card. Tape to the head on the long edges.

Working the design
5 Paste newspaper strips and apply a layer all over the cat. Leave to dry. Apply 3 more layers, leaving each one to dry before working the next.

6 Apply two layers of pasted tissue to smooth the surface.

7 Paint the entire cat with white emulsion.

8 Decorate the cat with acrylic colours. When dry, give a final coat of diluted PVA adhesive.

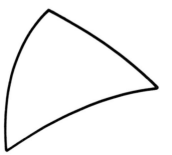

Trace this ear shape, cut 2 from card.

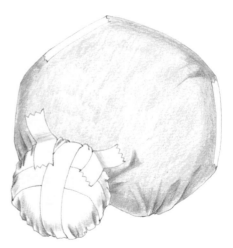

Tape the head and crumpled tissue to the body.

Black and white cat

Cat-lovers will treasure this life-like model – it makes an ideal gift for both children and adults. The basic structure is a plastic soft drinks bottle shaped with newspaper-stuffed plastic bags.

Materials

2 litre plastic soft drinks bottle
Plastic covered garden wire
Florist's stub wires
Clear adhesive tape
Plastic shopping bags
Newspaper
Wallpaper paste
Tissue paper
PVA adhesive
Acrylic paints

Preparation

1 Cut the bottom 4in (10cm) from the plastic bottle.

2 Trace the outlines for the wire armatures. Bend the thicker wire to the shapes of the tracings.

3 Fit the two wire shapes together and tape the wire ends to the bottle.

4 With thin wire, build up the head, twisting the wire round the thicker wire to hold the shape.

5 Stuff plastic bags with newspaper and arrange the bags over the bottle to shape the cat's body. Tape in place.

6 Roll a sheet of newspaper diagonally to form the tail. Tape to the body.

7 Cut 2 pieces of card 3 × 4½in (7.5 × 11cm) for legs. Roll into 1in (2.5cm)-diameter tubes. Stuff the bottom end of the tubes with screwed up paper for the feet. Flatten the other end of the tubes. Tape the legs to the body.

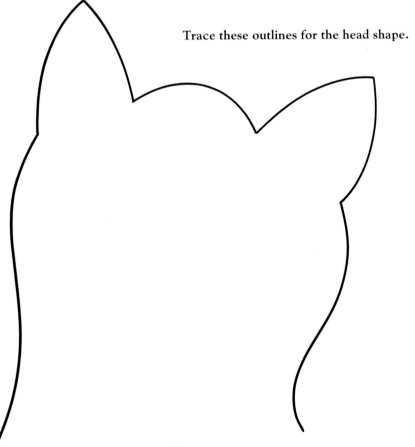

Trace these outlines for the head shape.

Working the design

8 Cover the entire cat with pasted strips of newspaper. Leave to dry.

9 **Shaping the face** Paste larger strips of newspaper and apply to the face to build up the muzzle. Take your time over this stage and do not try to do too much shaping in one session. Leave the work to dry out between each application.

10 Stand the finished cat on a piece of card and draw round the base. Cut out the shape and glue to the underside of the cat.

11 Paste pieces of tissue paper all over the cat and base to smooth the surface.

12 Brush 2 coats of PVA adhesive over the cat.

13 Trace the eye shapes on thin card and use them to position the eyes. When you have them in the right place, trace round the outlines and paint in the eyes.

Fit the wire shapes together, tape to the bottle. Tape newspaper-stuffed plastic bags to the bottle to shape the body.

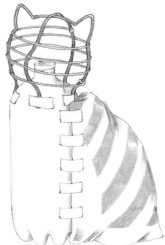

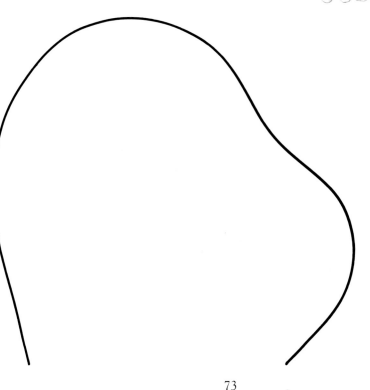

FOUR

Party Time

❧

Happy snowman

This jolly fellow would make an attractive party table centrepiece but as there is quite a lot of paper pulp work in this project, allow about a week to complete it.

Materials
Cardboard tube
Newspaper
Clear, sticky tape
2 cups of mixed paper pulp (refer to
    Better Techniques)
White emulsion paint
Acrylic paints
PVA adhesive

Preparation
1 Roll a ball of newspaper and tape it to
hold the shape. Tape it to the top of the
tube.

2 Tear newspaper into 3in (7.5cm)-wide
strips. Roll up and tape. Tape to the sides
of the tube for arms.

Working the design
3 Using a knife and your fingers, apply
paper pulp all over the figure. Try and get
a thin, even layer, then leave to dry. Put
the figure in a warm place to dry. Paper
pulp must not be encouraged to dry
quickly or cracks will form.

4 Apply two more thin layers of pulp
then begin the modelling.

5 Build up the hat and then paste a
folded strip of kitchen roll paper round
for a band.

6 Using pulp, model the scarf and
buttons and a pointed nose.

7 When the snowman is dry, give it a
coat of white emulsion paint. Decorate
with acrylic colours. Coat with diluted
PVA adhesive.

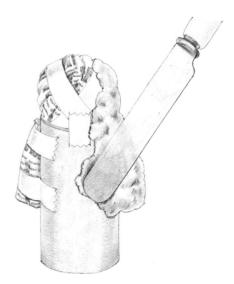

Tape the head and arms to the body. Using a knife, apply paper pulp to the figure.

Snow scene
Cut a large oval of stiff card.
Crumple some kitchen foil and stick
to the card, taking the edges over to
the underside. Mix a quantity of
paper pulp (refer to Better
Techniques) and spoon it on to the
card, heaping it slightly round the
edges. Aim for the effect of snow
drifts. Cut small sprigs of evergreen
and push them into the pulp before
it dries. Stand the snowman in the
middle. When the pulp is dry, paint
it white and sprinkle with glitter dust
before the paint dries. Add robins
and a small Christmas tree to the
scene.

Festive tree

Create this pretty table tree for your party decorations. Glistening beads hang from the branches for a Christmas look but you could also use tiny artificial flowers or small glass fruits or ribbon bows.

Materials
Florist's foam cone
Thin card
2 cups of mixed paper pulp (refer to
    Better Techniques)
Mixed wallpaper paste
Tissue paper
Kitchen paper roll
Acrylic paint
PVA adhesive
Silver florists' wire
Teardrop beads; small round beads

Preparation
1 Cut the card into 1½in, 2½in and 3½in
squares (3cm, 6cm and 8cm). Cut the
squares into triangles with convex long
sides.

2 Starting at the bottom, push large and
medium-sized triangles into the foam
tree, spacing them about ¾–1¼in (2–3cm)
apart.

3 Continue round and up the tree,
working first the medium-sized triangles
then the smallest at the top of the tree.
Insert one small triangle at the tip.

Working the design
4 Smear a little pulp on either side of the
branches to thicken them.

5 When dry, cover the tree and branches
with pasted pieces of tissue. Leave to dry
then apply two more layers.

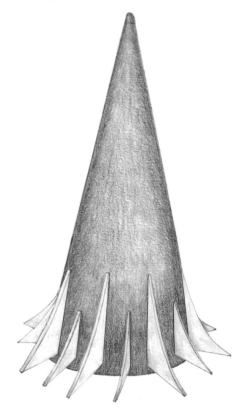

Push large and medium-sized triangles into the
cone.

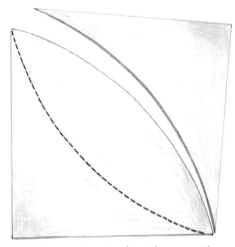

Cut card squares into triangles with convex sides.

6 Paint the tree green. Give a final coat
of diluted PVA adhesive.

7 Using a bradawl, pierce a hole in the
tip of each branch. Thread a short length
of wire through the hole. Thread on a

bead, twist the wire ends to secure.

8 Thread small round beads on wire and
join the ends to make a circlet for the top
of the tree. If you prefer, a star-shaped
silver bead could be stuck to the tree top.

Stars and moons

These decorations are based on florist's dry foam and, once covered with pasted paper and painted, they are hard-wearing and will last for many years. Children will enjoy helping to make them.

Materials
Block of florist's brown foam
Small balls of florist's brown foam
Florist's stub wires
Newspaper torn into small pieces
Tissue paper
Mixed wallpaper paste
Thin cardboard
PVA adhesive
Spray silver paint

STARS AND CRESCENTS
Preparation
1 Cut slices of foam from the block. Using a star-shaped and crescent pastry cutters, cut shapes.

2 Paste small pieces of tissue all over the stars and crescents, on both sides. Leave to dry.

3 Apply 3 layers of tissue, leaving each to dry before working the next. Use very narrow strips between the star points to keep the shape.

4 When the shapes are dry, spray with silver paint. Leave to dry, then spray the other side.

FULL MOONS
5 Work the foam balls in the same way, applying 3 layers of pasted tissue. Before the last layer is applied, cut small stars from thin card and stick them to the ball. Apply the last layer of pasted tissue, pressing the paper firmly on to the star shapes to show them in relief.

6 Spray-paint the balls silver.

Cut slices from the block. Cut stars with a pastry cutter.

Finishing
7 Cut small pieces of stub wire, bend into U-shapes. Bind the wire ends with narrow strips of pasted tissue. Leave to dry. Cut slits in the top of each of the ornaments, spread glue on the wrapped wire ends and push into the slit.

> **Star-shaped cutters**
> These are available with either five or six points. Crescents and stars could also be cut by hand.

Candlestick

This decorative candlestick is for display only and should not be used with a lighted candle. Once you have mastered the basic technique, you might attempt a branched candelabra.

Materials
Plastic-covered wire
Adhesive tape
Cardboard
Tissue paper
Mixed wallpaper paste
White emulsion paint
Gold and green paints; craft 'gems'

Preparation
1 Cut pieces of wire to 35in and 18in (87.5cm and 45cm) lengths. Twist the wires as shown to make the candlestick structure.

2 Cut a 2in (5cm)-diameter circle of card. Pierce a hole in the centre. Push on to the top of the candlestick stem.

3 Draw a 1in (2.5cm) diameter circle on paper. Cut a 1in (2.5cm)-wide strip of card to fit round the circle plus ½in (1cm). Lay round the circle, overlap the ends and tape. Glue to the candlestick card circle.

4 Trace the star shape on folded paper. Open the tracing and cut 2 from card. Tape the stars to the candlestick stem, one on each side.

Working the design
5 Tear tissue into strips 4in long by ¼in wide (10cm long by 6mm wide). Paste and wrap the candlestick structure. Leave to dry.

6 Paint the candlestick with emulsion paint.

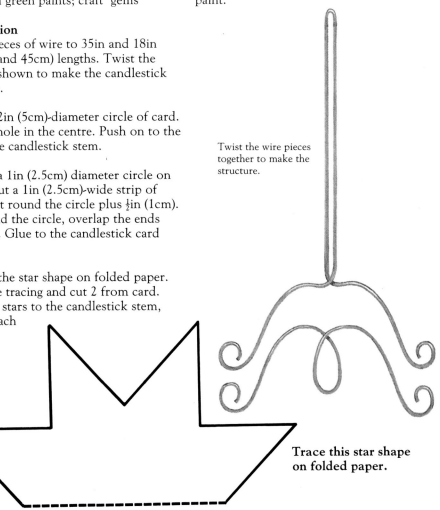

Twist the wire pieces together to make the structure.

Trace this star shape on folded paper.

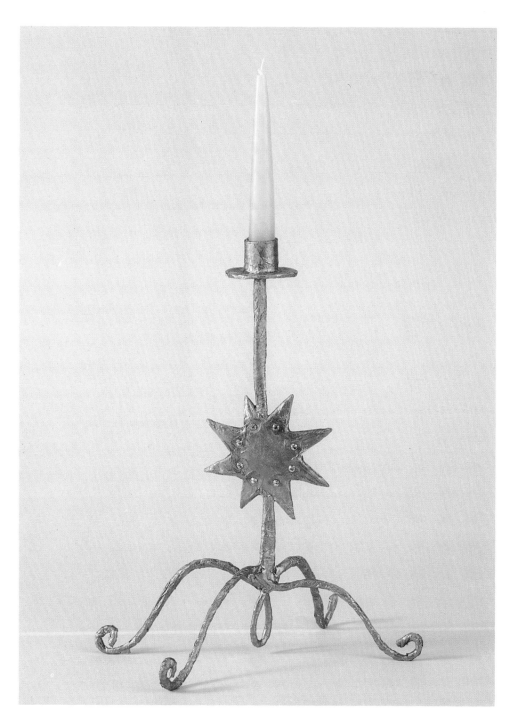

7 When it is dry, paint the candlestick gold. While the paint is still wet, dab green paint mixed with a little white all over the candlestick.

8 Pierce holes in the star shapes and stick the 'gems' in place. Clear gems have been used in the picture but coloured stones can be used if you prefer.

Serviette rings

Decorated with paper cut-outs, papier mâché
serviette rings make acceptable gifts for family and friends –
if you can bear to part with them.

Materials
Cardboard tubes (refer to Better
  Techniques)
Mixed wallpaper paste
Newspaper torn into strips
Tissue paper
PVA adhesive
Giftwrap, magazine illustrations, rub-on
  initials etc
White emulsion paint
Fine sandpaper
Water-soluble paste
Acrylic paint; gold paint
Matt varnish

Preparation
1 Make cardboard tubes of the desired
dimensions.

Working the design
2 Wrap the ring with narrow strips of
pasted newspaper until the edges are
rounded. Leave the work to dry between
layers.

3 Apply 2–3 layers of pasted tissue, to
smooth off the surface.

4 When the papier mâché is dry, give the
ring 2 coats of white emulsion paint.
When dry, rub down with fine sandpaper
until the surfaces on the inside and
outside are quite smooth.

5 Paint the ring with acrylic colours.

6 If the ring has an uneven surface after
painting, rub down again to smoothness.

7 Using fine, curve-bladed nail scissors,
cut motifs from thin paper. Paste round
the ring using water-soluble paste.

8 Press the motifs with a finger tip to
squeeze out any excess paste. Clean the
edges with a dampened cotton wool bud.
Leave to dry.

9 Spray the ring with fixative and leave
to dry.

10 Using a good-quality, soft-bristled
brush, apply a thin coat of varnish to the
outside of the ring. Suspend the ring on a
spoon handle to dry.

11 Apply more coats of varnish to the
ring, allowing each coat to dry before
applying the next, until the edges of the
motifs cannot be felt with a finger nail.
Between 5–6 coats may be needed.

12 Finally, varnish the inside of the ring.

Press a blob of Plasticine to the spoon handle, rest
the serviette ring on it to dry.

84

Man-in-the-moon

Hang the moon where there is a draught so that it turns in the current of air – or suspend the decoration where it is reflected in a mirror. For Christmas, you might make some matching silver stars.

Materials
12in (30cm) square of thick card
1 cup of mixed paper pulp (refer to
    Better Techniques)
Tissue paper
Mixed wallpaper paste
Black acrylic paint
Silver paint
Silver reel wire

Preparation
1 Cut a 10in (25cm) circle from the card.

2 Draw the moon's face from the graph pattern and transfer to the card. Cut out.

Working the design
3 Spread a thin layer over one side of the moon shape. Leave to dry.

4 Spread a layer of pulp on the other side and leave to dry.

Use this star shape if desired.

5 With the face looking to the right, use pulp to build up the features. Do not attempt too much modelling in one session. Take your time and allow each application to dry before starting again.

6 If cracks appear, fill them with more pulp. If the moon begins to warp as it dries, put weights on the ends.

7 Finally, apply 2 layers of pasted tissue paper to smooth the surface.

8 Paint the moon black on both sides. When dry, dip a piece of cloth in silver paint and rub all over the raised surfaces so that the black shows through. Pierce a hole at the top of the moon and thread silver wire through. Twist the end.

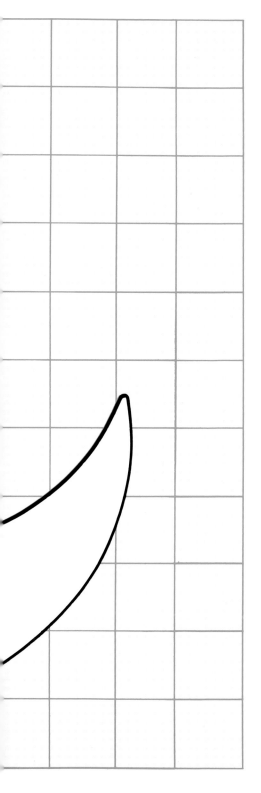

Working with graph patterns

Making your own patterns from graph patterns is not difficult although it can look daunting at first sight. You need the following materials and equipment for pattern making.

● Dressmakers' squared paper: this comes in different scales. Choose the one specified in the pattern.
● Tape measure and ruler.
● Medium-soft pencils.
● A flexible, plastic ruler for drawing curves.

To begin: Study the pattern and count the number of squares, first across the top edge and then down one side. Check with the scale. This tells you the dimensions of the area you will need on squared pattern paper. Draw this area.

With a pencil, number the squares on the graph pattern, across the top edge and then down one side. Number the squares on the squared pattern paper in the same way.

Using a ruler, and working from the graph pattern, copy any straight pattern lines. Still working from the graph pattern, mark any key points on the curved lines. Join up these points to complete the outline of the pattern.

Man-in-the-moon: scale 1 sq = 1in (2.5cm).

Christmas box

A storage box for jewellery or keepsakes can be created from any plain cardboard box using newspaper layering. This box has been decorated with holly leaves and berries for a festive look.

Materials
Cardboard box with lid
Newspaper torn into small strips
Kitchen paper roll
Mixed wallpaper paste
Tissue paper
Scraps of thin cardboard
Small beads
PVA adhesive
White emulsion paint
Acrylic paints; gold paint

Preparation
1 Set the lid on the box and pencil round the edges of the lid.

Working the design
2 Paste newspaper strips round the sides of the box up to the pencilled line and on the bottom, overlapping the strips. Leave to dry.

3 Apply strips to the outside of the lid but do not wrap the strips over to the inside or the lid will not fit on the box later. Leave to dry.

4 Work the box again, this time with strips of kitchen paper. Leave to dry and work 7 layers in all, alternating between newspaper and kitchen paper.

5 In the same way, work a total of 4 layers on the lid.

6 Finish both the box and the lid with tissue strips to give a smooth finish to the surface and the edges.

7 Try the lid on the box. It should go on easily and the papered surfaces should line up.

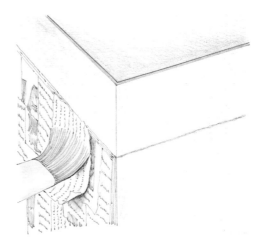

Apply newspaper strips only to the pencilled line.

Decoration
8 Cut holly leaves from thin card. Stick in place on the lid with the berries, using PVA adhesive.

9 When dry, paste tissue paper over the leaves and berries, brushing the tissue into place so that the decoration shows through clearly.

10 Paint the whole box with 2 coats of white emulsion paint.

11 Finish the box and decoration with acrylic paints and gold paint.

Gold and lace box

Round boxes are not difficult to make and lend themselves to all kinds of exciting decorative techniques. Cotton lace has been applied to the finished box and then painted gold.

Materials
Strip of soft, pulp cardboard
Thin card
Tissue paper
Mixed wallpaper paste
Clear, sticky tape
White emulsion paint
Wide, cotton lace
Gold paint
PVA adhesive

Preparation
1 Wet the cardboard strip and set it into a mug or cup so that it fits. Leave to dry in a warm place. The strip will have formed a tube. Trim away the overlap. Butt and tape the edges together.

2 Cut a circle of thin card to the diameter of the tube for the base. Cut another circle about ⅛in (3mm) larger for the lid. Cut a strip of thin card to fit round the tube loosely for the lid sides and tape to the circle of card.

3 Tape the base piece to the bottom of the tube.

4 Put the lid on the box and adjust the fit if necessary. Mark the edge of the lid with a pencil. Remove the lid and work the box part first.

Working the design
5 Apply small pieces of pasted newspaper over the outside of the box, up to the pencilled line. Leave to dry.

6 Apply a second layer, this time of pasted tissue pieces, but only up to the pencilled line. Leave to dry. Work another 3 layers up to the pencilled line.

Set the wet strip in a mug to dry. Butt and tape the short ends.

7 Apply a layer of tissue all over the box, taking the tissue over the top edge to the inside. Brush the tissue into the rim

92

formed by the earlier layers, to set the pasted tissue into the crease. When dry, apply a second layer. Paste tissue over the inside of the box.

8 Paste small pieces of newspaper over the outside of the lid. When dry, apply 2–3 layers of tissue, taking the last layer over the edge of the lid to the inside. Paste tissue over the inside of the lid.

9 Paint the box and lid with white emulsion paint, inside and out.

10 Stick the lace round the box, butting the ends.

11 Paint the box and lid with gold paint.

12 Give the box and lid a final coat of PVA adhesive.

Valentine keepsakes

Make a lace-edged heart to send to someone you love on this special day. The hearts can be hung for a wall decoration or will make an attractive accessory on a side table.

Materials
Thin card
Mixed paper pulp (refer to Better
 Techniques)
Newspaper
Tissue paper
Mixed wallpaper paste
Acrylic paints
Gathered lace edging
Paper lace doily
Ribbon

Preparation
1 Trace the heart shape and cut from thin card.

Working the design
2 Build up the heart with paper pulp. Smooth off the surface and leave to dry.

3 When dry, apply small pieces of pasted newspaper all over the heart. Leave to dry.

4 Apply 3 layers of pasted tissue all over the heart, leaving each layer to dry before working the next.

5 Paint the heart on both sides.

6 Stick lace round the heart, joining the ends at the top. Cut pieces from the paper lace doily and stick over the edge of the lace.

7 Tie a small ribbon bow and stick to the front of the heart. Make a ribbon loop and stick to the top of the heart, just behind the ribbon bow.

**Trace the heart shape,
cut from card.**

94

Better Techniques

With simple techniques and a minimum of equipment you can make your own bowls, plates, mirror frames, boxes and toys. Here you will discover the best methods for papier mâché and all you need to know about paper, card, paste and paint.

MATERIALS AND EQUIPMENT

Papier mâché, which literally means 'chewed paper', can be worked in various ways. Two techniques are in this book, layering and pulp work. The two most important materials you will be using are paper and adhesive.

PAPER

Newspaper has been used for most of the projects in this book but it is by no means the only paper that can be used. Almost any type of strong paper can be used for the foundation work – computer print-out paper, discarded letters and envelopes, typing paper – anything that comes to hand and which you can obtain in quantity. Old newspapers are, of course, a traditional favourite for papier mâché as these are readily available, cost nothing and are easy to handle. In this book, newspaper has also been used to make paper pulp.

Kitchen roll paper This is useful for building up work quickly. If kitchen paper is alternated with newspaper in layering, you can see if the surface being worked has been completely covered.

Tissue paper When layering or modelling is completed, tissue paper is used to smooth off the surface ready for undercoat painting. Tissue can also be used to add texture to a surface. Soft, paper handkerchiefs can also be used for the final layer.

Decorative papers Giftwrap can be used for decorating an object, either torn into strips for layering or for motifs. Tissue and crêpe paper are available in wide colour ranges and interesting effects can be achieved with these. Scraps of coloured paper from magazine pages often provide unusual patterns and textures which can be used as a decorative finish.

CARDBOARD

In this book, cardboard has been used to make basic structures and for surface decoration. In every instance, the cardboard has been throw-away waste.

Cardboard throw-away waste is ideal for papier mâché. Corrugated card, transit cartons, cereal boxes and fruit packing are all easily available.

Thin cardboard Where this has been recommended, cardboard of the weight and flexibility of cereal packets is required.

Thick cardboard When rigid card is required, cartons used for transit packaging of canned goods etc have been used. Suitable cartons are usually obtainable from supermarkets.

Corrugated card This is also freely available from supermarkets.

Pulped paper packing This useful material is used in packing fruit and comes pre-formed to take the shape of the fruit.

ADHESIVES

Wallpaper paste Cellulose wallpaper paste comes as granules which are mixed with water. Mix paste beforehand in order to allow time for the grains to swell. Use it at the strongest proportion and dilute it as required. Some wallpaper pastes have a fungicide in them and thus may not be suitable for children to use. Wash your hands frequently when working with these pastes.

PVA adhesive PVA is a multi-purpose, easy-to-use adhesive which can be used both as a glue and a varnish. Although white, PVA dries transparent and, as a finish, gives a glossy, protective surface. It can be used full strength or diluted with water.

Latex adhesive This is thick and white and comes in jars or tubes. It is specifically for sticking fabric, paper and card but should be used very sparingly.

Clear adhesive For working with paper and card, a clear, quick-drying, non-trailing adhesive is essential.

Water soluble paste This is available in jars and squeeze containers and is semi-opaque. It is safe for children to use, under supervision, and spills or smears can be removed with water.

Flour and water paste This is ideal for paper mâché layering and works as well as wallpaper paste. If salt is added, the paste will keep for several days. Between sessions, cover the paste and put in the refrigerator.

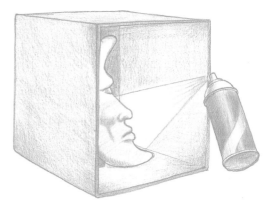

Use a large cardboard carton as a paint-spraying booth. Prop the object at an angle if required.

Spray adhesive allows you to spread adhesive over a large area of paper without dampening the surface. Spray adhesive should be used either in the open air or in a confined space (such as a spraying booth made from a cardboard box).

Flour and water paste
Mix plain flour and water together to a thick cream. Pour on boiling water, stirring. The paste will turn translucent and thicken. Dilute as required. Stir in a large spoon of salt to 6 cups of paste to keep it from hardening. Flour and water paste will keep in the refrigerator for several days.

PAINTS, DYES AND VARNISHES

Acrylic paints, which are water-mixable,
have been used for decorating all the
projects in this book. These paints dry
quickly with a silky, waterproof finish.
The shade ranges are large, and frosted
colours are also available. Wash brushes
immediately after use because acrylic
paint dries hard in a very short time.
There are special finishing varnishes for
acrylic paints.

Other paints used for crafts include
poster paints, water colours and designer
gouache. Model maker's enamel paints
and multi-purpose metallic paints can
also be used.

Emulsion paint Water-based white paint
is used as an undercoat before
decoration.

Gold and silver paints and spray paints
are needed for some projects.

Varnish for finishing and protecting
work can be gloss, satin or matt finish.

Paint brushes should include a range of
water-colour brushes and small,
household decorating brushes.

Dyeing pulp Cold water dyes or fabric
dyes can be used for colouring pulp and
interesting effects are possible. The dye
colour will lighten on drying.

OTHER MATERIALS AND EQUIPMENT

Tapes

For papier mâché, you will need masking
tape, clear, sticky tape and brown paper
strip tape.

Sandpaper

Fine sandpaper is used to smooth rough
edges on layered and pulp papier mâché.

Plastic-covered garden wire

This is used for making armatures under
papier mâché.

All the basic equipment needed for
papier mâché, bowls, spoons, knives,
buckets, cups and mugs etc, can be found
in the average kitchen (see Check list).

Cutting tools

Knives: You will need two kinds of craft
knives: a heavy duty knife, like a Stanley
knife or an X-acta knife for cutting thick
card, and a small knife, preferably a
scalpel, for thin card and paper. Use
straight blades, as these suit most tasks
and replace them often for the best
results. Needless to say, these knives
require care when in use. You should
always cut straight lines by lining up the
knife against a firm straight edge. Use a
metal rule for this rather than a plastic or
wood ruler, as these materials can easily
catch in the blade.

Scissors: You will need several pairs of
sharp scissors. Have a pair of fairly small,
easy-to-handle scissors with straight,
pointed blades for most cutting jobs, a
longer broad-bladed pair for general
cutting and manicure scissors with
curved blades for cutting round intricate
shapes.

Drawing aids

Drawing aids required include a pair of
compasses, a set square and a ruler with
small measurement markings. You will
also need paper clips, a stapler, a pencil
sharpener and a selection of HB and soft
pencils, coloured pencils and felt tipped
pens. A good quality eraser is helpful.

BASIC TECHNIQUES
Layering method
When you are using a dish or bowl-shaped mould, protect the work surface with newspaper then invert the mould over a suitable prop, like a can or mug – any object tall enough to raise the mould off the work surface and keep it stable.

Prepare the mould or structure. Tear paper into small strips about ½in (1cm)

Tear newspaper into long strips, then tear the strips into small squares and rectangles.

Rest the mould on a jar or can to raise it above the surface.

wide × 2in (5cm) long. This size strip will mould well round most curves. (For smaller or larger projects adapt the strip size.) As a guide, the strips should adhere to the mould without pleating or distorting.

Put some paste in a shallow bowl or dish. Start at the top of the greased

Preparing moulds
It is necessary to lubricate the mould before applying paper strips so that the finished papier mâché can be removed easily. Smear the mould surface liberally with petroleum jelly. If it is necessary to remove the papier mâché at any time during the drying process, re-grease the mould before replacing the work.

As an alternative method, dampen the first layer of strips instead of pasting them. The shell will then slip from the mould without difficulty.

mould. Use water only to dampen the strips and smooth each one in place, overlapping the edges slightly, to build a layer reaching downwards to the outside edge. Allow the strips to overlap the edge slightly as this can be trimmed later. Apply a second layer of strips, this time using paste and work the strips in the other direction. This helps to build a firm, strong web. Paint paste over the surface and smooth with your hands to remove any air bubbles. Do this after applying each layer of strips. Add another layer of glued strips, working downwards in the same direction as the first layer. Continue in this way until the layers are thick enough to hold the shape.

When you are working with newspaper strips, it is sometimes difficult to see whether you have completely covered the mould. If you use a different paper – such as kitchen roll paper – for alternate layers, you will be able to see when a layer has been completed.

100

Use a different paper for alternate layers. This helps to see when a layer has been completed.

Check list
Layering method
Paper, torn into strips
Mixed wallpaper paste
PVA adhesive
Paste container
Moulds
Petroleum jelly
Tissue paper
White emulsion paint
Household paint brushes
Varnish
Spoons for mixing
Crafts knives
Scissors
Metal-edged rule

Pulp method
Paper
Bucket
Fabric conditioner
Whiting or ground chalk
Mixed wallpaper paste
Linseed oil
Slotted spoon
Saucepan
Blender
Fine-mesh sieve
Petroleum jelly
Blunt knives, spoons, tools etc for modelling

Drying papier mâché
Papier mâché can take several days to dry so be patient if you want successful results. Keep the mould on the prop, and leave the work to dry naturally in a warm, airy place.

Fine finish
Some pieces may require a smooth finish before painting. When the last layer of newspaper pieces has dried, tear white tissue paper into small pieces and paste all over the surface. Leave to dry, then apply another layer. A third layer may be necessary if the newspaper surface was rather rough.

Removing work from the mould
To unmould a bowl shape, gently insert a thin knife, such as a palette knife, between the bowl and the mould and slide round to break any vacuum which may have formed. Gently twist the bowl and ease the papier mâché away and place on a work surface. Trim the uneven edge with scissors, or leave it in its natural state if you prefer. Check for any thin patches and build these up with extra strips. Leave to dry. Smooth any uneven patches with sandpaper.

Loosen the paper shell from the mould with a palette knife.

Trim the edges of the shell with scissors.

Working intricate shapes

If the structure you are working on has protruding corners or curves, cut down on the number of newspaper layers and work more final layers with tissue paper. Bowls or plates with a decorative edge, for instance, will retain their edges if narrow strips of tissue are pasted over them. Use the bristles of the paste brush to work pasted tissue into crevices and corners. Brushing pasted tissue can also be used to create a decorative finish. Tear fairly large pieces of tissue, paste the surface of the piece liberally and then pick up the tissue on the brush. As you paste it into place, allow creases and folds to form.

Work surface

The work surface is important. This should be at a good working height, flat and stable. You will require a protective surface to use over the work top, to protect it from cuts and scratches when using crafts knives. A sheet of thick card or board is a suitable protection but should be replaced frequently as the surface will become pitted from successive knife cuts.

Pulp papier mâché

The material used for this technique is usually made from torn newspaper boiled up with water and with adhesive added. Other types of paper can be used instead of newspaper – copy paper, typing paper, scrap notepaper etc. The finished pulp is slippery in texture and rather wet to the touch. Paper pulp is modelled with the fingers in a similar way to clay. It can be worked over or inside a mould or it can be modelled over a base to build up a surface or design. The secret of successful pulp work is to let the work dry very slowly.

When using a mould, smear petroleum jelly over the entire area. Spoon the pulp into the mould and press it well down to ensure a compact layer.

A drying period of several days should be allowed. Avoid using any means of speeding up the drying process as this may cause the papier mâché to crack or distort. If small cracks do appear while drying, fill these with more pulp, smoothing off the surface, then replace the papier mâché to dry once again.

When you are building up an area, such as features on a face or a decoration on a frame or dish, model by applying the pulp slowly. Allow each layer to dry before continuing the work.

Jelly moulds with interesting shapes are ideal for making pulp models. Press in the pulp firmly.

PAPER PULP

Materials
6 double sheets of newspaper (or similar quantity of other white paper)
$\frac{1}{4}$ cup fabric conditioner
7 large spoons of whiting or ground chalk
6 large spoons mixed wallpaper paste
2 medium-sized spoons linseed oil
4 medium-sized spoons PVA adhesive
Large saucepan

Preparation
Tear the paper into small pieces no larger than $\frac{5}{8}$in (15mm) square. Put the paper into the bucket and cover with water. Add the fabric conditioner. Leave to soak for 12 hours.

Method
Pour water and paper into a large saucepan and bring to a boil. Simmer for 30 minutes. The paper will begin to break up. If a dark scum rises to the top of the water, skim this off. Leave the mixture to cool. Working in batches, mix, using the blender. Strain the pulp into a sieve and press with the back of a spoon to remove as much water as possible. Transfer the strained pulp to a large mixing bowl. Stirring well, mix in the whiting and wallpaper paste, then the linseed oil and PVA adhesive. Mix thoroughly. The pulp is ready for use.

Dried paper pulp can be purchased, requiring only the addition of cold water. This is easy to use and ideal for children where only a small amount of pulp may be needed at a session. You may also find it useful when working on a modelling project over several days, mixing only what is needed each day.

Decorating papier mâché
After the last layer of smoothing tissue has been applied and has dried out, give the piece a thin coat of white emulsion paint and leave to dry. You may decide to apply 2 coats if the surface requires it. Acrylic paints, which are water-mixable and quick-drying, are ideal for painting papier mâché items but modeller's enamels, poster colours and even household paints can also be used. The painted decoration can be varnished with clear, polyurethane varnish or given a coat of water-diluted PVA adhesive. If the item is to hold liquid (such as a vase) then 3–4 coats of varnish should be applied both inside and outside.

If you cannot draw or paint, découpage is an ideal technique for decorating papier mâché. Paint the piece in a single colour. Cut motifs from colour magazines or from giftwrap. Paste them to the surface, using a water-soluble paste. Spray varnish all over. Leave to dry then apply several thin coats of varnish to the surface, leaving each coat to dry thoroughly before applying the next, until the paper edges cannot be felt with a finger nail. This is a very hard-wearing finish for items that will be handled a great deal.

To paint paper beads, thread them on a knitting needle, support the needle across mugs or jars.

SPECIAL PAPER CRAFTS
Cutting paper and card

To cut card, lay it flat on a protective surface. Draw the pattern outline directly on to the card. Use a set square and ruler to check right angles and parallel lines. Line up the straight edge against the line to be cut. Press the crafts knife against the metal edge, and firmly draw the knife towards you, keeping an even pressure on the straight edge to keep it still. Score the cutting line gently to mark it (and if only marking fold lines) then still with the straight edge in position, cut along the line again, pressing harder through the card. To cut round curves, mark the shape lightly with the knife point and cut round, making sure that the free hand is pressing firmly on the card to keep it still, and that fingers are not in line with the knife, should it slip.

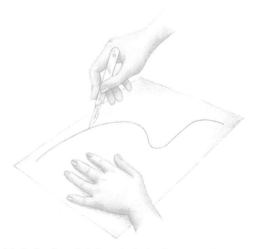

Mark the shape lightly with the knife point and then cut round.

When using scissors to cut paper shapes (such as when cutting out motifs for découpage decoration) it is sometimes desirable to soften the cut edge. To do this, hold the paper right side facing you and roughly cut round the required

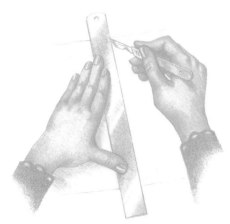

Firmly draw the knife towards you.

Pierce the corner with the scalpel point, draw it towards you.

To use a scalpel on paper, follow the same basic process. When cutting small shapes with right angles and tight curves, start by piercing the corner point of each shape with the point of the blade, and cut away from the corner, drawing the knife towards you. This should ensure neatly cut points.

shape, leaving a generous border round the main subject matter. Now hold the scissors blades at a slight angle away from you and cut round again at the required edge. By cutting the paper at an angle you create a bevelled edge, making the harsh cutting line less noticeable. Use curved manicure scissors, the blades positioned appropriately, to cut out very small shapes.

Use curved-bladed
manicure scissors to
cut out découpage shapes.

Pleating paper

Pleated paper responds well to papier
mâché techniques and is easy to make,
relying on careful measuring and accurate
folding. Cut a strip of paper to the
required depth. Use a set square to check
the right angle at one end of the strip and
a ruler and pencil to measure and mark
out equally spaced divisions along the
top and lower edge. Join these marks up
with a ruler and pencil, then gently score
along each line. Fold up the pleats. To
join pleats, simply overlap the ends by an
entire pleat, arranging the join so that the
edge on the right side is hidden in the
valley of the fold. Secure behind with
adhesive.

Join the marks in pencil, then score along each line.

Removing glues

Adhesive manufacturers will always
help with advice about solvents for
their products and some will supply
these solvents direct if you write to
them. In general, the first step in glue
first aid is to scrape off any deposit
and then proceed as follows:

Clear adhesive:

On skin, wash first, then remove any
residue with nail varnish remover.
On clothing or furnishings, hold a
pad of absorbent rag on the
underside, dab with non-oily varnish
remover on the right side.

Epoxy adhesive:

Lighter fuel or cellulose thinners will
remove adhesive from the hands. On
fabrics, hold a rag pad under the glue
stain, dab with cellulose thinners on
the right side. On synthetic fibres,
use lighter fuel.

Adhesive tape residue:

White spirit or cellulose thinners
may do it. Or try nail varnish
remover. Adhesives vary and you
will have to experiment.

Latex adhesive:

Lift off as much as possible before
the adhesive hardens. Keep the glue
soft with cold water and rub with a
cloth. Treat any stains with liquid
dry cleaner. Scrape off any deposits
with a pencil eraser.

Wallpaper paste:

Scrape as much paste from the fabric
as possible. Spread the fabric over a
bowl or dish and pour cold water
through the residue. Dab cold water
on any remaining stain.

With all adhesives, read the
manufacturer's instructions carefully
before use and have the necessary
solvents at hand to cope with
accidental spills.

CARD AND PAPER
Covering corners

Whether you are covering the sides of folders or boxes, you can achieve neat, professional looking corners by following one of the methods described here. The first, folded method is more suitable for thin papers. The second, cut and dart method can be used for thicker papers as bulk is reduced. It gives neat covered corners on the edges of thick card where it is sometimes difficult to avoid the card from showing through. However, if this does ever happen you can insert a little patch of matching paper over the corner, underneath the covering paper. Both of these methods use either a stick adhesive or a clear, quick-drying craft glue to secure the corners and overlaps.

Folded corners

Working on the reverse of the card, crease the overlap diagonally at the corner and stick the overlap on to the card. Crease the folded paper gently at the card edge and fold each overlap on to the card. Stick in place.

Cut and dart corners

Working on the reverse of the card, make a cut in line with each straight edge, then cut a narrow strip within that, tapering towards the corner of the card. Cut the overlaps away at each side. Gently apply glue to the centre strip and smooth it on to the card. Press the strip flat to mould the corner shape. Spread glue on the shaped overlaps and press on to the card.

Folded corner: crease the overlap diagonally on the corner.

Cut and dart corner: cut the overlaps away at each side.

WORKING WITH CRÊPE PAPER
Stretching and curling paper

The grain of paper can be used to advantage for moulding paper to a required shape and one of the easiest ways to shape paper is to gently stretch and curl it over a scissor blade. Most lightweight papers respond well to this treatment and especially crêpe paper and paper ribbon.

To stretch the paper, cut out the shape with the grain running in the direction to be stretched. Hold the paper in one hand and the open scissors blade in the other. Gently pull the blade across the underside of the paper, from the base to the tip of the shape. Repeat until the paper is curled sufficiently.

To stretch paper across its grain, to mould it into a rounded curve, as for

the cross about $1\frac{1}{2}$–2in (4–5cm) wide. Cut one edge into a fringe, cutting about $\frac{1}{4}$in (6mm) apart and on the true grain. Using a scissors blade, carefully curl each strip of the fringe over the blade. To form the flower centre, roll the fringe strip from the end. Alternatively, the strip can simply be gathered in the fingers.

Gently pull the blade across the underside of the paper to curl it.

making flower petals, cut out the required shape with the grain running opposite to the required stretch direction. Hold each side of the shape between thumb and fingers and gently stretch, stroking the paper sideways with the thumbs to mould it. The upper and lower edges of the shape can be further shaped by curling over a scissors blade if required.

When cutting crêpe paper into a fringe, as when making paper flower centres or stamens, cut strips of paper on

After cupping a petal, shape the edges by curling them over a scissor blade.

Children's fun with papier mâché

Working with papier mâché is child's play. Here are some ideas for children to try using both the pulp and layering techniques.

Masks

Work 2 layers of newspaper over a half of a balloon, supported on its side. Cut a segment from an egg carton for a nose. Tape in place. Work 4 more layers. Paint the finished mask, cut holes for eyes. Pierce holes at the sides for string ties. Stick on fringed crêpe paper or knitting yarn for hair, eyebrows, beards, moustaches etc.

Animal masks

These are great fun for carnivals. Begin by taping a food carton to the balloon to shape the muzzle. Paste 2 layers of newspaper strips over the balloon and carton. Cut out ears from stiff paper. Tape to the mask. Cut strips of paper and tape round the sides to widen the mask. After 6 layers, pierce the balloon. Remove the food carton. You may need to line the mask with 2 layers of pasted tissue paper. Cut the eye holes and pierce holes for threading through the ties. Paint the mask with white emulsion paint then decorate.

Fine fish

Cut 2 fish shapes from thin card. Tape the shapes together on the edges, leaving a gap. Stuff a plastic bag into the fish. Tape the gap to close. Tape on fins and a tail cut from stiff paper. Apply 3 layers of pasted newspaper. When dry, paint the fish.

Sheep toy

Inflate a small, long balloon. Paste newspaper strips all over the balloon. After 3 layers, roll strips of pasted paper and tape to the balloon for legs. Cut a segment from an egg carton and tape to the end of the balloon for a head. Apply 5 more layers of pasted newspaper. When dry, cut 2 slits near the nose for ears (this will burst the balloon). Paint the sheep all over with white emulsion paint. Cut thick white knitting wool into short lengths. Twist into curlicues and stick to the sheep's body. (Use strips of white kitchen paper if you prefer.) Plait wool for a tail. Stick to the end. Cut 2 card ears and stick into the slits. Paint the face and legs black.

Puppet heads

Stand a small plastic bottle or box on the neck of a soft drink bottle to support it. Work 3–4 layers of newspaper over the plastic bottle. Smear pulp all over then, when dry, model eyebrows, nose and mouth in paper pulp. Paint with emulsion paint. Decorate. Fold a fabric square in quarters, cut off the point. Stick the puppet neck into the hole. Try the puppet on the hand with the index finger in the bottle. Cut holes in the fabric for the thumb and third finger. Stick fringed crêpe paper or knitting wool to the head for hair.

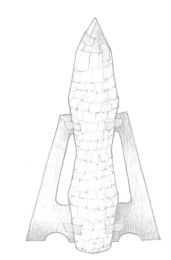

Space ship

Tape 2 yoghurt pots together, rim to rim. Tape 2 more. Tape them all together so 4 pots are standing up. Work 2 layers of newspaper strips all over. Cut a 4in (10cm)-diameter circle of cereal packet card. Cut in half, tape the edges to make a nose cone. Tape to the top of the space ship. Cut 2 long fins from card, tape to the ship sides. Work 4 more layers of newspaper all over. Paint with emulsion paint and then decorate with felt tipped pens or poster paints.

Fun fruit

Grease fruit – apples, pears, oranges or bananas – all over with petroleum jelly. Work all over with very small pieces of pasted newspaper. Work 4 layers. Cut round the paper shell very carefully and lift the 2 halves from the fruit. Tape or stick the halves together again. Paste tissue paper over the join. Paint with emulsion paint. Paint the fruit.

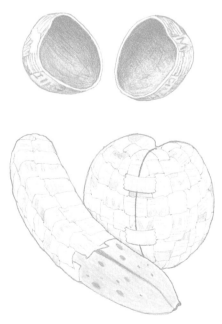

Fringed candle holders

Cover a small jar with pasted newspaper pieces. Apply 3 layers. Coat with emulsion paint. Cut thick, cotton fringe to fit round the top of the jar. Dip the fringe in PVA adhesive. Stick round the jar, spreading the fringe out. Leave to dry.

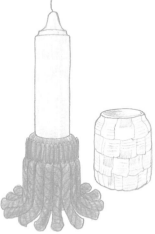

Mosaic place mat

Cut a rectangle of thick white board. Cut coloured areas from quality magazines. Cut the paper into strips, then into uneven squares and rectangles. Paste the squares on to the card in a pattern or in an abstract all-over design. Stick coloured adhesive tape round the edges. Coat with PVA adhesive to seal the surface.

For a decorative edge, form some balls of paste-soaked tissue. Place them round the tray edges. Paste small strips of tissue over the balls, dabbing the tissue between the balls with the brush. Paint.

Classic candle holder

Collect a group of containers – jars, plastic containers with lids, small cans, cottage cheese pots etc. Arrange one on another, cutting pieces of thick card to go between. Stick or tape the pieces together. Cover with pasted newspaper pieces. Paste thin strips round the narrow areas. Apply 6–7 layers. When dry, coat with 2 layers of emulsion paint. Draw freehand designs on the candle holder. Glue string or braid to the surface in patterns. Paint the candle holder with acrylic paints. Finish with clear varnish.

Make music!

Start a papier mâché band.

Maraccas: Layer over small balloons. Cut the shell in half, tape a wooden handle between the 2 halves, put in dried beans and tape the halves together. Apply 2 more layers of papier mâché.

Tambourine: Cut a 2in (5cm)-wide strip of card 18in (45cm) long, tape the ends together. Paste 4 layers of newspaper strips inside and outside. Pierce 4 holes on the edges. Thread metal buttons on cotton, tie 3 through each pierced hole.

Bongo drum: Tape greaseproof paper over the open top of a large tin. Cover the tin and top surface with 2 layers of pasted newspaper strips. Paint all the instruments with white emulsion paint then decorate in bright colours.

Savings pig

Work 2 layers of newspaper over a large grapefruit or a ball. Roll pasted strips of kitchen paper for four, short stubby legs. Tape to the top side of the pig. Roll strips for a flat snout. Tape to one end of the pig. Complete the layering. Apply 6–8 more layers. Cut all round the pig, and remove the fruit or ball. Cut a money slit in the top half. Stick the halves together, paste tissue over the join. Paint the pig with emulsion paint then paint with acrylic paint. Finish with painted eyes and 2 large, felt ears.

Snake

Cut 2 egg cartons into pieces so that you have 12 segments. Cover each segment with pieces of pasted, white kitchen paper. Pierce a hole on the opposite edges of each segment. Paint the segments. Thread on strong cotton or thin string with a large bead between each segment. Tie a knot at both ends of the cotton and leave 10in (25cm) of cotton at the head end and 4in (10cm) at the tail end. Tie the long cotton to the top end of a stick, tie the short end halfway down the stick. As you wave the stick the snake will wiggle.

> For a group project, children can make a farmyard. Spread pulp on a board, make farm buildings from card and paper layering. Keep the farm to the scale of toy, plastic animals.

Carnival hats

Three basic shapes will make a variety of hats.
Pillbox: Tape a ring of thin card to fit the head. Cut a circle of card to fit the ring, tape together.
Skull cap: Work the shape over a balloon. Cut the shell to fit the head.
Cone: Cut a half-circle on stiff paper, tape into a cone to fit the head.

A brim on the pillbox makes a soldier's cap. Use just the ring for a crown and cut the edge decoratively. A wide brim on the skull cap makes a picture hat. Add a brim to the cone for a witch's hat. Cover the basic structures with papier mâché then paint with emulsion paint. Decorate with painted designs or tissue flowers, rosettes etc.

Doll's house furniture

Use papier mâché techniques for making furniture from small card or wooden boxes. Stick small boxes together, tape on pieces of card as required. Paste 2 layers of small pieces of newspaper all over. Finish with a layer of white tissue paper. Paint with white emulsion. Decorate with cut-outs from colour magazines, pieces of coloured cartridge, fabric snippets or paint with poster or acrylic colours.

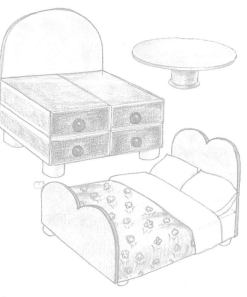

Useful addresses
Dry paper pulp can be obtained from the
following suppliers:

James Galt & Co Ltd
Brookfield Road
Cheadle
Cheshire SK8 2PN
UK

Louise Kool & Galt Ltd
1147 Bellamy Road, Unit 6
Scarborough, Ontario
M1H 1H6
Canada

Selegiochi sri
Via Fumagalli 6
20143 Milan
Italy

James Galt & Co Inc
63 North Plains Highway
Wallingford
Connecticut 06492
USA

**Kangaroo Trading
Holdings PTY Ltd**
PO Box 1055
Brookvale
New South Wales 2100
Australia